Records of Dettingen Parish Prince William County Virginia

1745-1802

Vestry Book
1745-1785

Minutes of Meetings of the
Overseers of the Poor
1788-1802

Indentures
1749-1782

Historic Dumfries Virginia, Inc.

HERITAGE BOOKS
2007

HERITAGE BOOKS

AN IMPRINT OF HERITAGE BOOKS, INC.

Books, CDs, and more—Worldwide

For our listing of thousands of titles see our website
at
www.HeritageBooks.com

Published 2007 by
HERITAGE BOOKS, INC.
Publishing Division
65 East Main Street
Westminster, Maryland 21157-5026

International Standard Book Number: 978-0-7884-4450-6

RECORDS OF

DETTINGEN PARISH

PRINCE WILLIAM COUNTY, VIRGINIA

VESTRY BOOK, 1745-1785

MINUTES OF MEETINGS OF THE
OVERSEERS OF THE POOR, 1788-1802

INDENTURES, 1749-1782

Library of Congress Number 76-28678

Historic Dumfries Virginia, Inc.
Dumfries, Virginia
1976

TABLE OF CONTENTS

PREFACE

The publication of this volume was undertaken by Historic Dumfries Virginia, Inc., as a bicentennial project designed to make readily available to the public the historically important records of Dettingen Parish and thereby to stimulate interest in local history and to encourage further research on the people, events and places of Prince William County, Virginia.

The present volume complements previously published parish records of the region and time:

George H. S. King, The Register of Overwharton Parish, Stafford County, Virginia, 1723-1758, and Sundry Historical and Genealogical Notes (Fredericksburg, Va.: George King, 1961), (out of print); Philip Slaughter, The History of Truro Parish in Virginia (Philadelphia: George W. Jacobs and Co., 1908), (out of print); and Minutes of the Vestry, Truro Parish Virginia, 1732-1785 (Lorton, Virginia: Pohick Church, 1974). The vestry book of Hamilton Parish is missing; Bishop Meade records that it had been placed in the office of the Clerk of Fauquier County and "... there torn up, page after page, by clerks or others, for the purpose of lighting cigars or pipes."

Dettingen Parish was established by law in 1744 by division of Hamilton Parish, which, in turn, had been taken from Overwharton Parish. Dettingen conformed to the present boundaries of Prince William County except for some divergences on the northern and western sides.

The Parish took its name from a Bavarian village, scene of a British victory in the War of the Austrian Succession in the preceding year. Prince William Augustus was wounded in the battle and shortly after, in recognition of his service, was promoted to lieutenant general.

A chapel of ease, established in the upper portion of Overwharton Parish in 1667 on Quantico Creek, became the parish church of Dettingen. The old church, known both as Quantico and as Dumfries, was in existence at the time Dettingen Parish was formed, and it may be that there was also at that time a wooden chapel in existence near present day Brentsville, which was known variously as Broad Run, Cedar Run, and Slaty Run. As recorded in the Dettingen Parish minutes, new churches were constructed soon after the establishment of the Parish, but both had fallen to ruin by the early 1800's.

Dettingen Parish, was, like other Virginia parishes in the pre-revolutionary era, both a civil and an ecclesiastical jurisdiction. Among other duties, the Vestry levied taxes for the support of the Church and of its police and local government functions, administered poor relief, processioned the boundaries of lands, educated and apprenticed poor children, and exercised police powers relating to

the personal conduct of the people within the Parish. These vestries
served as training grounds for the members in broader public service
in county, commonwealth and national governments. The nature and
extent of the exercise of these public responsibilities are clearly
visible in the minutes of Dettingen Parish which cover the period
1745-1785.

Although the Church in Virginia was not formally disestablished
until 1799, the functions of support of the poor and processioning
of lands, and the power to tax to finance these functions, were taken
from the vestries in 1786 and assigned to the newly formed Overseers
of the Poor. The Dettingen records show the operational effects of
separation of church and state functions which took place over the
last quarter of the 18th century.

The minutes of the Vestry and of the Overseers of the Poor
contained in this volume are transcriptions of the original documents.
The original spelling (and mispelling), capitalizations and
punctuation have been retained, with only minor changes such as in
punctuation and spacing deemed essential to aid the reader and the
researcher. The page numbers of the original manuscript are shown in
brackets or parentheses in this volume.

The indentures are summarized, but a few texts are shown in full
as samples or variations of the customary contents and format. In
summarizing the indentures all information contained in the text
identifying both master and servant is presented, except that unless
otherwise indicated in the summary, it is to be assumed that both
are residents of Dettingen Parish and Prince William County. Provisions
of the indentures regarding obligations of the master for instruction
of the servant are set forth in full in the summaries, but the
servant's obligations to the master and the master's responsibilities
to the servant for support and for payments in money or kind at the
end of the apprenticeship are omitted.

The publication of the Dettingen Parish records was initiated and
carried forward as a project of the Research Committee of Historic
Dumfries Virginia. The Committee gratefully acknowledges the efforts
of those who generously gave of their time, in the spirit of public
service, without compensation or reimbursement of expenses, to make
the publication of this volume possible, particularly

To Barbara Kirby of Dumfries, an organizer of Historic Dumfries
Virginia and its first President, who, as a member of the Committee,
undertook the search for the records, succeeded in locating them in
the Virginia State Library in Richmond, procured a microfilm of the
manuscript and transcribed the entire volume into typescript,

To Anne P. Flory of Bel Air Plantation, the current President of
Historic Dumfries Virginia, who moved the project forward in
innumerable ways, including proofing the entire first typescript from
the microfilm,

To Mrs. Martha E. King of Manassas, who gave generously of her
genealogical expertise, especially in the planning of the summari-
zation of the indentures, and,

To Ann H. Moore of Gaithersburg, Maryland, whose enthusiasm for history and historical research, led her to undertake the many demanding tasks involved in production of photo-ready copy, including essential editing, preparation of the index, and final typing and proofing.

The contributions of these volunteers is multipled by the fact that all the proceeds of sales of this publication, except for actual photo-offset printing and binding costs, will accrue to Historic Dumfries Virginia for use in future historical projects of public interest.

<table>
<tr><td>Bel Air Plantation</td><td>Dr. William E. S. Flory</td></tr>
<tr><td>Prince William County</td><td>Chairman, Research Committee,</td></tr>
<tr><td>May 13, 1976</td><td>Historic Dumfries Virginia, Inc.</td></tr>
</table>

VESTRY BOOK, 1745-1785

Prince William ss.

Pursuant to an act of Assembly of this Colony for Dividing the
Parrish of Hamilton into two Distinct Parishes, I, John Grant Gent.,
Sheriff of the County of Prince William, on the twenty second and
twenty third Days of may Anno: 1745 Caused the freeholders &
Householders of the Parish of Detingen to meet me at William Balis
within the Said Parish of Dittengen, then and thereby the free Consent
of the freeholders and Housekeepers of the said Parish of Dettingen
Elected the following Persons to Serve as Vestrey men of the said
Parish of Dettingen (Viz): Vallentine Peyton, Francis Searson,
William Butler, John Deskin, Moses Linton, Lewis Renno, Richd.
Blackburn, Isaac Farguson, Charles Ewell, Anthony Seale, Benjamin
Grayson & John Baxter.   [Signed] John Grant Sheriff.

Met at the Vestrey house at Quantico Church in Dettingen Parish
on the 1st day of June 1745 & after Being Duely Swore According to Law
& Subscribed the Test as followeth (Viz):
We, Vallentine Payton, Francis Searson, William Butler, John
Deskin, Moses Linton, Lewis Renno, Richard Blackburn, Isaac Farguson,
Charles Ewell, Anthony Seal, Benja. Grayson & John Baxter, Doo
Declare that we Doo Believe there is not Any Transubstantiation in
the Sacrament of the Lords Supper or in the Elements of Bread & wine
at or After the Consecration thereof by An Person whatsoever.
Vallentine Payton, Francis Searson, William Butler, John Deskin,
Moses Linton, Lewis Renno, Richard Blackburn, Isaac Farguson, Charles
Ewell, Anthony Seal, Benja. Grayson & John Baxter Was Entred
Vestreymen of Dettingen Parish.

[2] At A Vestrey held at Quantico Vestrey house in Dettingen
Parish the 1st day of June 1745
Present: Capt. Vall. Peyton, Mr. Fras. Searson, Mr. Wm. Butler,
Mr. John Deskin, Mr. Moses Linton, Mr. Lewis Renno, Collo. Richd.
Blackburn, Mr. Isaac Farguson, Capt. Chas. Ewell, Mr. Antho. Seal,
Majr. Benja. Grayson, Mr. John Baxter:
Ordered that the Late Church Wardens of Hamilton Parrish, Mr. John
Diskin, and Capt. Valla. Peyton, Deliver in their Former Accots. (not
Legally Proved) Upon Oath to the Next Vestry.
Ordered that all persons that make up Any Accots. for the time to
Come with this Vestrey they Make them upon Oath.
Ordered that Capt. Vall. Peyton & Mr. William Butler be Church
Wardens for the Insuing year, they Haveing Taken the Oaths According
to Law.
Ordered that Burr Harrison be Clerk of this Vestrey, he having
been first Sworn.
Ordered that Mr. James Scott be Received as Minister of this Parish
on this Condition, that he shall Remove Into this Parish & there
Reside as Soon as the Vestrey will get a Glebe & Houses for him.
Ordered that Mr. John Bryant be Continued Reader at Quantico Church

& Mr. Machen at Broad Run Chapell tell the Laying the Parish Leavie.
Ordered that the Clerk of this Vestrey Enter on the Register of this Parish The Governours Letter & the Comesaries which was this day Offered to the Vestrey by the Reverend James Scott.
[Signed] John Deskin, Valla. Peyton, Isaac Farguson, Wm. Butler, Anthony Seale, Fras. Searson, Moses Linton, Benja. Grayson, Lewis Renno, Chas. Ewell, R. Blackburne, John Baxter.

Williamsburg Apl. 26th 1745

Gentlemen:
As your Parish is at Present unprovided with a minister, I Recommend to your Approbation & Choice the Reverend Mr. Scott who is in my Opinion a Man of Discretion Understanding & Integrity & ev'ry way Qualifyd to discharge that Sacred Office to your Satisfaction. I am

Gentlemen
Your Affect. Friend
And Humb. Servt.
William Gooch

Gentlemen,
I hope & Believe that your Parish will be Worthily Supplied by the Reverend mr. James Scott, his Merit haveing been Long Known to you I need not Enlarge Upon it that you may be Greatly Benefited by his good Life & Doctrine, Mutually Happy with Each Other, & that all the Souls, Committed to his Charge may be Saved is the Daily Prayer of,

Gentlemen,
W. and M. Col.   Your Most Affectionate
Apr. 26 1745   Humble Servant
                                William Dawson.

[4] At A Vestrey held at the Vestrey house of Dettingen 11th. July 1745
Present: The Reverend James Scott, Vallentine Peyton, William Butler, Churchwardens; John Diskin, Anthony Seal, Lewis Renno, Issac Farguson, Charles Ewell:
Ordered that the Church Wardens buy Linnen to make a Surplass for Each Church.
Ordered that Vallentine Peyton & Charles Ewell Settle the Accot. of Phyals Balla. of a Legacy to Quantico Church due from the Estate of John Gregg Decd. & Upon the Exor. Refuseing to Settle & Pay the Same, to Bring Suit.
[Signed] James Scott, Minr.; Vall. Peyton, Wm. Butler, Isaac Farguson, Chas. Ewell, Antho. Seale, Lewis Renno, John Deskin.
[5] At a Vestrey held at Quantico Vestrey house in Dettingen Parish October 14th 1745
Present: James Scott, Ministr.; Capt. Vall. Peyton & Mr. Wm. Butler, Churchwds.; Fras. Searson, Mr. John Baxter, Moses Linton, Lewis Renno, Richd. Blackburn, Anto. Seale, Benja. Grayson, John Deskin, Chas. Ewell, Isaac Farguson, Vestry Men:

DETTINGEN PARISH

	Dr. Tobo.
To Part of the Revd. Jas. Keith's Sallerie	4064
To 6 months Sallerie to the Revd. Jas. Scott nett cash	8320
To Wm. Champney for Being Clerk in Hamilton Parish 4 months	433
To John Bryant Clerk for Hamilton Parish	216
To Do. for Dettingen Parish 6 months	650
To Mrs. Margt. Farrow for Being 6 months Sexton in Hamilton Par.	200
To Do. for Do. in Dettingen Parish	200
To Mr. Peter Waggener's Claim Against Dettingen Parish	48
To Thos. Woodup a Poor man 6 months for Hamilton Parish and 6 months for Dettingen Parish	700
To Mary Justise a Poor Woman Do. Do.	500
To Wm. Bennett for Keeping a Blind man Do. Do.	800
To Mr. Wm. Butler's Accot. for Elements for the Church	80
To Capt. Val. Peyton's Accot. for Do. 50 lbs. tobo. & Do. for Hamilton Parish	100
To Wm. Bland for 2 Leavies Overcharged Last Year to his Son	33
To John Hogan for Being Sexton 6 months	250
To Do. for Do. for Hamilton Parish 6 months	250
To Burr Harrison for Keeping the Register 6 months	250
To John Tippitt for Work done at Quantico Church	100
To James Calk for Keeping Saml. Scurrey a Poor man	500
To Mr. Robt. Bogle's Accot. for Linnen for Surplasses	1333
To Mrs. Eliza. Cooke for Makeing 2 surplases @ 150 lbs. Tobo.	300
To Danl. Feagan for Keeping a Bastard Child one year	800
To Capt. Vall. Peyton for Tobo. Overpaid Last year more than the fraction	13
To Capt. Chas. Ewell for Books for the Parish	541
[6] To Issac Farguson for Keeping Eliza. Horman a Poor woman	400
To Tobo. left in the Church Wardens hands for to Agree with Workmen to Build a Gallerie in Broadrun Chapple	2500
To Tobocco to be Left in the Churchwardens hands to be sold for cash to pay for glass for the Church & Chapple	2000
To 6 Percent for Collecting 25581 lbs. Tobacco is	1535
To a Fraction Left in the Church Wardens hands	240
Cr. by 977 Tythables at 28 lbs. Tobo. p. Poll is	27356

Ordered that the Church Wardens Collect from Each Tythable Person the sum of twenty Eight Pounds of Tobacco, it Being the Next Parish Leavie for this Present year & that they Enter into Bond for the Payment of the severall Claims & Due Performance of the Several Order of Vestrey Unto Burr Harrison Clerk of this Vestrey.

Ordered that John Florance be Exempted from Paying the Parish Leavie.

Ordered that A Bastard Child Liveing at Danl. Feagans be Bound to the Said Danl. Feagan by the Churchwardens According to Law.

Ordered that the Church Wardens Agree with Workmen to make...two windows at Broadrun Chapple & one in Quantico Church and Alter the Pews at both Churches & Build one new one in Quantico Church.

Ordered that John Bryant be Continued Clerk of Quantico Church tell the Laying of the Next Parrish Leavie.

[7] Ordered that John Peyton Junr. be Clerk of Broad Run Chapple tell the Laying of the Next Parish Leavie.

Ordered that John Hogan be Continued Sexton at Broadrun Chapple tell the Laying of the Next Parish Leavie.

Ordered that John Carr be Sexton at Quantico Church tell the Laying of the Next Parish Leavie.

Ordered that Majr. Thomas Harrison have the Liberty of Building a Gallerie for the Use of himself & Family in Broadrun Chapple not Discommodeing any of the Pews in the Chapple.

Ordered that Majr. Thomas Harrison & Mr. Wm. Butler meet at the next Vestrey in Hamilton Parish in Order to Joyn the Vestrey in setling the Late Churchwardens Accots. of Hamilton Parish.

[Signed] James Scott, Ministr.; Val. Peyton, Wm. Butler, R. Blackburn, John Diskin, Lewis Renno, Isaac Farguson, Benja. Grayson, Anto. Seale, John Baxter, Moses Linton, Fras. Searson, Chas. Ewell.

[8] At a Vestrey held at Quantico Vestrey house in Dettengen Parish the 4th day of October 1746

Present: Mr. James Scott, Ministr.; Capt. Val. Peyton, Mr. Wm. Butler, Churchwds.; Colo. Richd. Blackburn, Mr. Fras. Searson, Mr. John Baxter, Mr. Lewis Renno, Mr. John Diskin, Majr. Chas. Ewell, Mr. Issac Fergason, Mr. Moses Linton, Mr. Anto. Seale:

DETTINGEN PARISH

	Dr.
	1b. Tobo.
To Revd. Jas. Scott Minister	16000
To Do. for Cask	640
To Mr. John Bryant Reader	1200
To Mr. John Peyton Do.	1200
To John Ker Sexton	500
To John Hogan Do.	500
To Burr Harrison Clerk Vestr.	500
To Thos. Weedup a Poor man	500
To Mary Justice a Poor Woman	500
To Wm. Bennett for Keeping a Poor Man	200
To Capt. Val. Peyton Churchwds. Accot.	205
To Simon Lutrell for work done	250
To Thos. Young Sherf. Accot.	236
To Mr. Geo. Junkir.son for work done	2525
To Mr. John Graham for 140 Sqs. of Glass	2333
To Mr. Wm. Thompson for work done at Broadrun Chaple	540
To Mr. Wm. Butler Church wds. Accot.	400
To Ben Parker for keeping Richd. his Bror.	600

To Mr. Timo. Thornton for Cureing Mary Horman   700
To Mr. John Canterbury for a Leavie Over Charged   28
[9] Cr. By Capt. Val. Peyton Churchwds. accot.   2240
                                                                         ‾‾‾‾‾
                                                                         27917
Dr. to 6 p. Ct. on 27917   1675
                                                                         ‾‾‾‾‾
                                                                         29592
Cr. By 975 Tythables @ 31 p. Pole is   30225
                                              Fraction is   633

    Ordered that Mr. Chas. Ewell & Mr. Wm. Butler be Churchwardens for
the Ensueing year they haveing Taken the Oaths According to law & that
they Collect from Each Tythable Person in this Parish the Sum of Thirty
One Pounds of Tobacco it Being the next Parish Leavie for this Present
year & that they Enter into Bond for the Payment of the Severall Claims
& that they Perform the several Other Orders.
    Ordered that the Clerks be Continued at 1200 lbs. Tobo. each till
the Laying of the Next Parish Leavie.
    Ordered that the Sextons be Continued @ 500 lbs. Tobo. each till
the Laying of the Next Parish Leavie.
    Ordered that the Church Wardens bind three Molatto Children the
Issue of Patt Fullam to Colo. Richd. Blackburn.
    Ordered that Mr. Charles Ewell Imploy an Atturney or Atturneys
in the suit of Mr. Byrn agt. this Vestrey & that he buy a Large Prayer
Book for Quantico Church.

    [10 Illegible, 11] At A Vestrey held at Quantico Vestrey house in
Dettingen Parrish the 8th day of June 1747
    Present: Mr. Wm. Butler, Majr. Cha. Ewell, Churchwardens; Capt.
Valla. Peyton, Collo. Richd. Blackburn, Mr. John Diskin, Collo. Benja.
Grayson, Mr. Fras. Searson, Mr. John Baxter, Mr. Lewis Renno, Mr.
Issac Farguson, Mr. Moses Linton, Vestrey Men:
    Ordered that the Church Wardens of Dettengin Parrish Apply to the
Church Wardens of Hamilton Parrish for to get Advertisements signed
by the said Churchwardens for the sale of the Old Glebe of Hamilton
Parrish on the fourth Monday in October Next at Prince William Court
house According to the Act of Assembly.
    Ordered that the Churchwardens of this Parrish give Notice for all
Persons Inclineable to Sell Land for a glebe, that they Meet at the
Next Vestrey in October for the Laying the Parrish Leavie.
    Ordered that the Succeeding Churchwardens bind unto Mr. Wm. Butler
a Molatto garle Named Judith born of the Body of Ann Reaves the 27th
day of January 1746, According to Act of Assembly.

    [12] At A Vestrey held at Quantico Vestrey house the 9th day of
November 1747
    Present: Mr. James Scott, Ministr.; Mr. William Butler, Collo.
Benja. Grayson, Churchwds.; Mr. John Diskins, Mr. Moses Linton, Mr.
Isaac Forguson, Mr. Antho. Seale, Mr. Lewis Renno, Mr. Fras. Searson,
Capt. Valla. Peyton, Vestrey Men:

DITTENGIN PARRISH

Dr.

To the Revd. James Scott Minisr.	16000
To Do. for Cask	640
To Mr. John Bryant Reader at Quantico	1200
To John Peyton Do. at Broad run	1200
To John Carr Sexton at Quantico	500
To John Hogan Do. at Broad run	500
To Burr Harrison Clk. Vestrey	500
To Thomas Woodup a Poor man	500
To Mary Justice a Poor Woman	500
To William Bennett for Keeping a blind Man	800
To Isaac Farguson for Burying Eliza. Horman	400
To William Murfey for Burying John Gaskins	300
To Cuthbt. Harrison for keeping a Bastard Child	800
To James Calk for keeping a Do.	800
To Phillo. Watters for keeping a Do.	800
To William Champ 1 Leavie Overcharg'd	31
To William Coram 1 Do.	31
To Benja. Parker for keeping his Brother Richard	600
To John Coles for 1 months bord for Henry Owins 50	050
To Peter Waggener Clks. Accot.	96
[13] To Thos. Youngs Accot.	240
To Doctr. John Briscoe acct. for cureing Hen. Owins & 1 pr. Shoes	1240
To be Leavied & Left wth. the Church Wardens to be Sold for Cash & £ 25 to be Paid Collo. Harrison	4000
To 6 pct. for Collecting	1844
	33572

Credt.

By Mr. William Butler's Churchwds. Accot.	1003
By 1041 Tithables at 32 lbs. p. is	28107
	29110
Left in the Churchwardens hands	04462
	33572

Order'd that the Church wardens Collect from Each Tythable Person thirty two Pounds of Tobacco being the Parrish Leavie for the Present Year.

Order'd That John Peyton be Clerk of Quantico Church tell the laying of the Next Parish Leavie & that he tend Every Sunday.

Order'd that Joseph Thurman be Clerk at Broadrun Chappell tell the Laying of the Next Parrish Leavie & that he tend Every Sunday.

Order'd that Thos. Bristoe be Sexton at Broad run Chappell tell the Laying the Next Parrish Leavie.

Order'd that the Proportion's that were made at the Vestrey on the 7th day of October Last be not Entred in the Register of this Parish.

Order'd that Collo. Thomas Harrison be Paid one hundred & thirty five Pounds for four hundred Acres of Land on Quantico run & if less in Proportion but if More we have the whole.

Order'd that the Churchwardens see Collo. Thos. Harrison's Land Surveyed & that they Receive Deeds for the Same with a General

Warrante in Name of Vestrey.

[14]   At A Vestrey held at Quantico Vestrey house in Dettingen
Parrish the 9th day of October 1747
   Present: Mr. William Butler, Churchwarden; Collo. Richd.
Blackburn, Mr. John Diskin, Capt. Valla. Peyton, Mr. Fras. Searson,
Mr. John Baxter, Mr. Antho. Seale, Mr. Moses Linton, Mr. Lewis Renno,
Mr. Isaac Farguson, Vestrymen:
   Order'd that the Churchwardens bind to Cuthbert Harrison a Bastard
Child the Issue of Hannah Murfey According to Law.
   Order'd that the Churchwardens bind to James Calk a Bastard Child
the Issue of Easter McGuire According to Law.
   Order'd that the Churchwds. bind to Philloman Watters a Bastard
Child the Issue of Judith Obryan According to Law.
   Order'd that William Butler, John Diskin, Antho. Seale & Isaac
Farguson View the Lands of Philloman Watters, Thos. Renno, Thos.
Harrison, William Ashmore, Cuthbert Harrison, Collo. Benja. Grayson &
Mr. George Mason which the have Offer'd to Sell to the Vestrey for a
Glebe & that they Make their Report to the Vestrey of the Quantity &
the Prices Offer'd at.
   Order'd that the Setling of the Parrish Leavie be Refer'd tell
the Next Vestrey for this Parrish.
   Order'd that the Person Appointed by the Vestrey held the 8th day
of September 1747 begin to Procession the Lands According to the
Orders of that Vestrey the Last of October & Procession & Make their
Reports & finish the Same by the Last of March According to Law.
   Order'd that Collo. Benja. Grayson & Mr. William Butler be Church
Wardens for this Parrish this Ensuing year & that Collo. Benja. Grayson
take the Oathe According to Law at the Next Vestrey.

   [15]   At a Vestry Held at Quantico Vestryhouse the 12th Day of
Aprill 1748
   Present: Mr. James Scott, Minr.; Collo. Benja. Grayson, Church
Wdn.; Collo. Richd. Blackburn, Capt. Valla. Peyton, Mr. Lewis Renno,
Mr. Anth. Seale, Mr. John Diskin, Vestmen.:
   Order'd that Capt. Wm. Triplet be Vestmn. instead of Mr. Wm.
Butler Dec'd
   Order'd that Mr. Antho. Seale be Church Warden instead of Mr. Wm.
Butler Dec'd & Sworn Accordingly.
   Order'd that Mr. Antho. Seale & Mr. John Diskin Demand the Money
of Mr. John Greggs Estate Due to Quantico Church and if Refus'd to
Bring Suit.
   Order'd that Collo. Benja. Grayson Pay half the Quitrents Due of
the late Glebe out of the fines of the Parish if Rec'd.
                                                     Adjd.

   [16 blank, 17]   At a Vestrey held at Quantico Vestrey house the
4th Day of November 1748, Mr. James Scott, Minister; Collo. Benja.
Grason, Mr. Anthony Seal, Church Wds.; Collo. Richard Blackburn, Mr.
Lewis Reno, Mr. John Deskin, Mr. John Baxter, Mr. Isaac Farguson,
Vestreym'n.:

DETINGEN PARRISH

Dr.

To the Reverend James Scott Minister	16000
To Do. for Cask	640
To John Peyton Reader	1200
To Joseph Thurman Reader at Broad Run	1200
To John Carr Sexton at Quantico	500
To Thomas Brister Sexton at Broadrun	500
To Burr Harrison Clk. Vestry	500
To Ballance John Briant in the year 1747	100
To Thomas Weedup a Pore Man	700
To Mary Justice a Poor Woman	500
To Wm. Bennett for Keeping a Blind Man	800
To Benjaman Parker for keeping his Brother Richd.	600
To Mr. Peter Waganer Clks. Acct.	58
To James Whaley 4 Leavies Twice Charg'd at 32 lbs. p. Laie	128
To Moses Congrove 2 Leavies Twice Charged @ 32 lbs. p. Do.	64
To Thomas Bland 2 Do. Twice Charged @ 32 p. Do.	64
To Morrise Neale 3 Do. Do. @ Do.	96
To Robert Whitliff 6 Do. Do. @ Do.	192
To John North for Glassing the Windows & other Work Done at Quantico	240
[18] To Thomas Reno for Mending a Diall at Broad Run	...
To Lewis Reno for Work Done at Quantico Church	150
To Robert Hedges for Buring James Wilson	300
To George Junkinson for Work Done at Quantico	...
To Wm. Chester for Keeping Thomas Folley	550
To Mr. James Nisbett for Curing Thomas Folley	1340
To Mr. James Scott Minister 4 Bottles Clarrot Wine @ 40 pr. Bol.	160
To William Bailis 1 Leavie Over Charged	...
To Collo. Benja. Grason cash 4/11d.	
To Thomas Young for Going to King Wm. Court house as Evedence	...
To Mr. Foushe Tebbs for Sheriff's Fees	...
To the Sexton for Washing the Surpoless 100 lbs. Each Sext.	200
To Collo. Thos. Harrison & Thos. Machen Claims	2000
	29330
Credt. By the chwd. Acct.	420
	28910
To 6 pr. Ct. on 28910 for Coling.	1734
	30644

Credt. By Ant. Seale Chwd. acct.	⅄ 1: 5: 0	
To Collo. Benj. Grason		4:11
	⅄ 1: 0: 1	

Ordered that Collo. Benjaman Grason & Anthony Seal to be Continued Church Wardens Tell the Next Parish Leavie be Lavd.

Ordered that the Church Wardens Collect from Each Tithable Person Thirty Pounds of Tobacco being the Parish Leavy for the Preasent year.

Ordered That Wm. Jones be Exempted from Paying the Parh.
Ordered that Philla. Watters Senr. be Exepted from Paying The
Parrish Leavy.
[19]   Ordered That John Tackett shall have 200 lbs. of Tobo. at
the Laying of The Next Parrish Leavy for Boarding Sarah Davis One year.
Ordered that Mr. Robert Wickliff, Captain Bertrend Ewell, Mr. Wm.
Tebbs be Vestrey men in Room of Capt. William Triplett, Dec'd
Moses Linton & Freancis Searson, Remd., in Detingin Parish.
Ordered that John Peyton be Continued Clerk Quantico Church Tell
the Laying the Next Parrish Leavie.
Ordered that Joseph Therman be Continued Clk. Broadrun Chaple Tell
The Laying the Next Parish Leavey.
Ordered that the Church Warden Pay to Collo. Thomas Harrison & Thos.
Machen there Respt. Claims out of The Two Thousd. Pounds Tobo. Leavied
for that Purpose & to Settle it in there Acct. at the Laying the next
Parish Leavie.

[20]   At a Vestrey held at Quantico Vestrey House 21st Day of Novr.
1748
Present: Collo. Benjaman Grason, Mr. Antho. Seal, Churchwds.;
Collo. Richard Blackborn, Capt. Vale. Peyton, Mr. Isack Ferguson, Mr.
Lewis Reno, Mr. John Baxter:
Ordered that the Processioners Returns be Register'd according to
Law.
Ordered that a Base Born Garle named Letice the Eshew of Spence be
Bound to John Peyton Junr. Tell She Comes to the Age of Eighteen.
[Signed] Benjaman Grason, Anthony Seale, Church Wardens; Ricd.
Blackburn, Val. Peyton, Lewis Reno, John Baxter, Isaac Farguson.

[21]   At a Vestrey held at Quantico Vestrey House the 4th Day of
November 1749
Present: Mr. Anthony Seale, Mr. Robert Whitley, Churchwd.; Mr.
James Scott Minister; Collo. Benjn. Grason, Collo. Richd. Blackborn,
Mr. John Diskins, Mr. Lewis Reno, Capt. Vall. Peyton, Mr. Isaac
Ferguson, Collo. Thomas Harrison, Batt. Ewel, Vestreyn.

To the Revd. James Scott Minister	16000
To Do. for Cask	640
To John Peyton Reader at Quantico	1200
To Joseph Thurman Reader at Broadrun	1200
To John Carr Sexton at Quantico	500
To Thos. Brister Sexton at Broadrun	500
To Burr Harrison Clk. Vestrey	500
To Do. for Recording the Processioners Rept.	400
To Joseph Butler for Makeing a Cofing for Thos. Weedup	125
To Mary Weedup for her Husband	582
To Mary Justice a pore Woman	500
To Wm. Bennet for keeping a blind man	800
To Benjaman Parker for keeping his Brother Richard	600
To Mr. Wagener Clks. Acct.	24
To John Bland one Leavie over Charg'd	30
To Robt. Bland one Do.	30
[22] To Doctr. John Briscoe Acct.	2400

To Tobo. for to be sold for to Discharge the Lawers Fees
in the Suit of George Byrn   2000
To John Jackson for Burying a pore man   400
To Do. for a Leavi Over Cnarged   30
To John Carr for keeping a pore man   320
To John Tacket for keeping of Sarah Davice   200
To Do. for finding Sarah Davice Close   240
To Doctr. Nisbet for acct.   1086
To John Carr for keeping & Washing the Surpiles   100
To Thos. Bristoe for keeping & Washing the Surpiles   100
To Collo. Benja. Grason Church wardens acct.   337
To Burr Harrison for Ballance of his Acct. for Buring
Willm. Whitting   75
To the Collecter of the Last Parish Levie fractn.   44
To Mr. James Scott for two yeares rent   1260
                                                            ‾‾‾‾‾
                                                             31471
To 6 pr. St. on 31471   1889
                                                            ‾‾‾‾‾
                                                             33360
Credt. By 1105 thyables at 31 pr. pole is 34255 fractn.   897

Ordered That Mr. Seale Churchwarden Collect from Each thyable
person the Sum of thirty one pounds of tobacco it being the Parish
Leavie for this present yeare.
Ordered that the Chwds. pay out of the fraction in there hands, to
Iaac Greggrey four hundred & fifty pounds tobacco for nursing an
Orphand Child.
[23] Ordered that Mr. Anthony Seale & Mr. Robert Whitley they
being first Sworn be Churchwarden for the Prest. yeare.
Ordered that John Peyton be Continued Cler. at Quanticoe Church
till the Laying of the Next Parish Leavie.
Ordered that the Churchwarden Set up advertisemt. for Workemen
to Come in & bring there Plans & Preporsals to agree with the Vestrey
for Building Gleeb Houses at Easter Tuesday next.
Order'd that Mr. Geo. Britt hath Libertey to Buld a Galerey at
the Loerend of Quontico Church for his use.
Ordered that the Corlector pay Mr. James Nisbet out of the Fraction
in his Hands 200 pound Tobac.
Ordered that the Churchwardens Bring Sute agt. John Grigg Exer.
for the Money Due from him to Quantico Church.

A a Vestrey Held this 27th Day of November 1749 at Prince Wm.
Court House
Present: Mr. James Scott, Miner.; Anthony Seal, R. Blackburn,
Val. Peyton, Benja. Grason, John Deskins, Lewis Reno, Batrand Ewell,
Vestreymen:
Ordered that Ricd. Blackburn, Benja. Grason & Lewis Reno, Gent.
be trusted to receive a Conveyance of three Hundred & Ninty-five acres
of Land Sold by Thos. Harrison Gent. as a Gleeb for Detingen Parish.

[24] At a Vestrey held at Quantico Vestrey house the 8th Day of
April 1750
Present: Mr. James Scott, Minester; Mr. Robt. Whitley, Mr. Antony
Seale, Churchwds.; Collo. Richard Blackburn, Collo. Thos. Harrison,

Captn. Valentine Peyton, Mr. Isack Forguson, Collo. Benja. Grason, Mr. John Deskins, L. Reno, Mr. John Baxter, Vest.Men:
Ordered that the Church Wardens Set up Advertisemt. for Workmen to Com in to undertake the Bulding of the Gleabe houses According to the Dementions this Day Set Down, on the Seventh Day of June next, When ye Vestrey is to Meet to receive there Preporsals.
Order that the house be Bult of the following sizes: A Dwelling hous be 40 feet Long & 20 foot Wide, A barn 40 foot Long & 20 foot Wide With a 10 foot Shed for a Stable,...A Dary 10 foot Squair And a Smokehous of the Same Demention. A Garden 100 foot squair A hen hous Lettle house & Cornhouse.

[25] At A Vestrey held a Quantico Vestrey house the 19th day of Novr. 1750
Present: Mr. James Scott, Minister; Mr. Anthony Seale, & Mr. Robt. Whitlife Chwds.; Collo. Thomas Harrison, Mr. Lewis Reno, Mr. John Baxter, Mr. John Deskins, Mr. Wm. Tibbs, Collo. Benjaman Grayson, Mr. Batterand Ewell, Collo. Richard Blackburn, Vestrey Mn.:

DETINGEN PARISH

Dr.

To the Revd. James Scott Minister	16000
To Do. for Casqe	640
To John Peyton Reader at Quantico	1200
To Jseph Thurman Reader at Broad Run	1200
To John Carr Sexton at Quantico	500
To Thos. Brister Sexton At Broad Run	500
To Burr Harrison Clk. of the Vestrey	500
To Phillaman Waters Senr. for Burrying Sarah Davis	400
To Mary Weedup a poor Woman	250
To Wm. Jones	31
To Henry Peyton for Sheriff fees	64
To Moses Bland for keeping a blind Man 18 Months	1000
To Benjam. Parker for keeping his Brother Richd. Parker	600
To the Revd. James Scott for keeping a Base Born Child	300
To Do. for 2 Gallons Wine 20/	
To Wm. Bennett for keeping a blind man	800
To Collo. Thomas for keeping a pore Man	400
To Do. for Drawing...Deeds for the Gleebland	200
To Nicholass Snoe a pore man	530
To Mr. Robt. Wickliff 2 Galls. Wine 20/	
To Do. for 4 yards Check Linnen for a Pore Child	40
To Levied for Bulding in Part of the Gleeb houses	15000
	40655
[26] To 6 pr. Ct. collecting 40655	2439
	43094
Cr. By 1141 Thyables @ 38 pr. p. is	43358
	43094

fract.

43094

264

DETINGIN PARISH   Cr.
By Mr. Anthony Seale   ₤ 13: 4: 9

Ordered that the Collectors Collect from Each tythable Person Thirty Eight Pounds of Tobo, it being the Parish Leavie for this Present yeare,

Ordered that Mr. Robt. Wickliff being Appointed Collecttor with Given bond wth. Security & that he & Mr. Lewis Reno be Church Wardens for this Prest. Year.

Ordered that John Peyton be Continued Clerk at Quantico Church till the Laying the Next Parish Leavie.

Ordered that Joseph Thurman be Continued Clerk at Broad run Chaple till the Laying the Next Parish Leavy.

Order'd that Thomas Bristoe be Sexton at Broad Run Chappell.

Ordered that John Carr be Sexton at Quantico Church.

Ordered that Mr. Seale pay out of the Money in his hands for two prayer Books that are sent for.

Ordered that Mr. Seale pay the remd. of the Money in his hands to the undertaker of the Gleabe Worke Which is to be taken out the Sum of tobacco agreed for by the Vestrey at 12/6 pr. Ct. after Bond and Good Security Given.

[27] Ordered that the Clarks Attend to Read prayers Every Sunday.

Ordered that the Church Wardens Pay out of the Fraction Left in there Hands One hundered Pounds of Tobacco to Each Sexton for Washing the Surpolaces.

As it is agreed by the Vestriey that the Vestrey hous is Ill convt. Ordered that a Vestrey hous be built at the Most Convenant Place by Burr Colberts plantation for holding of Vestreys for the Parish of Dittingin & that the Church wardens agree With Workemen to buld the same, to which Order Coll. Richard Blackburn, Coll. Benjaman Grayson, Robert Wickliff, & Mr. John Baxter Enter there Decent.

Ordered that the fifteen Thousand pounds of Tobacco Levied this Day be Paid to John Diskins he giveing Bond with Good and Sufficiant Security for Sundrey Buildings to be Done on the Gleabe Plantation in the Parish of Detengin accord. to a Scheeme given in this Day & that the Said John Diskin have agreed to finish the said Buildings in a good & Sufficiant Workman Like manner by the 25 of December In the yeair of our Lord 1752 with the Futer allowance of twenty three thousand five hundred Pounds of tobacco to be Levied at two Payments Equaley Each at the Laying the two next parish Levies in Case the said Bulding is fully Compleated by that time, and that the Ballance of Cash in the Church Wardens hands at the Laying this Present Levie be paid to the said John Deskins Deducting the same at 12/6 pr. Ct. out of the a Bove Mentioned Sum. The Said John Deskins is Ordered to Give bond & Security to the two Church Wardens for the time Being & Collo. Richd. Blackburn, Capt. Batrand or any three of them & that the Same are appointed [28] viewers of the said Buldings. Battrand Ewels Desent against the a Bove Order.

[29] At A Vestrey hed for Quantico Vestrey house the 9th Day of Aprill 1751

Present: Mr. James Scott, Minister; Mr. Robt. Wickliff, Mr. Lews. Reno, Cws.; Mr. Anthony Seale, Mr. John Baxter, Mr. Isack Forgason, Mr. Wm. Tibbs, Vestreymn.:

Whereas John Deskins Gent. Who at the Vestry held for this Parish in Novr. last did agree With the sd. Vestrey Men to buld a Glebe house, Kitchen and Garden and Office for the Sum of thirty Eight thousand five hundred pounds of tobacco for the Preformance of Which agremt. he Was to Give Bond & Security but Refused to Give the Bond & Desired to be Excused, the Vestry Mett Considering his Incompasity of Doing them do agree he Shall be Excused & Doe therefore Order that the Fiftee Thousand Pounds of tobacco levied last Novr. for Gleeb houses be Paid the Revd. James Scott, he Giveing Bond and Sufficient Security for bulding Sundry houses and a garden on the Gleeb of this Parish According to a Scheem given in Novr., and the Said James Scott agrees to finish the Said Buldings in a good and workman like Manner by the first of May in the yare 1753 for Which he is to have the further a lowance of twenty fore thousand pounds of Tobo. to be Levied....

Ordered also that the Ballance of Each that Shal be Left [30] in Mr. Seales hands after Paying the Orders of Last Vestrey Shall be Paid to the sd. James Scott & Deducted Out of the Above Tobacco at 12/6 pr. Ct.; the said James Scott also agrees to Give bond and Security to the Two Church Wardens & Coll. Ricd. Blackburn, Capt. Batrd. Ewel or any three of them Who are Likewise to Receive Such Bond.

Ordered that John Dalgam be free from Paying Psh. Leavy till he recure his helth again.

At A Vestrey Held at Quantico Vestrey house the first Day of October 1751
Present: Robert Wickliff & Lewis Reno, C.W.; Thos. Harrison & Richard Blackburn, Benja. Grason & Antony Seale & Battrand Ewel, Vestreymn.:
Ordered that James Nisbet Gent. be appointed Vestreyman in the Roome of Valentine Peyton Gent. Decd.

[31] At a Vestrey held at Quantico Vestry house the 9th Day of Decr. 1751
Present: the Revd. James Scott, Robt. Wickliff, Lewis Reno, Churchwd.; Collo. Benja. Grayson, Mr. Antho. Seale, Mr. John Diskin, Mr. Wm. Tebbs, Mr. James Nisbet, Collo. Thos. Harrison & Bertrand Ewell, Vestymen.:

DETINGEN PARRISH	Dr.
To the Revd. James Scott	16000
To Do. for Cask	640
To Do. for Making it Neat	640
To John Peyton Reader at Quantico	1200
To Joseph Thurman Reader at Broad Run	1200
To John Carr Sexton at quantico	600
To Thos. Brister Sexton at broad run	600
To Burr Harrison Clerk Vesty.	500
To John Carr for keeping Richd. Jones a blind man	600
To Benja. Parker for keeping his brother Richd. Parker	600
To Nicho. Snow a Poor man	530

```
To John Webb a poor man                                    300
To Capt. Ewell for burying James Purcell a poor man        250
To Walter Seales for burying James Mulrunce                400
To Wm. Tackett for keeping a base born Child on
    month                                                   67
To Majr. Waganer for Copying a List tithables Nett          96
To Mason Bennett over Paid three Leavies                   114
To the Revd. James Scott Levied for building a Gleabe    12000
To Wm. Bennett for keeping a blind man                     800
To Ann Murphey for burying Thos. More                      160
[32] To Collo. Thos. Harrison for keeping a poor man       400
To Mr. James Nisbett for Medisons for John Delgarn         605
To Levied for building two Churches                      20000
                                                         -----
                                                         58302
To a mistake in Adding up the Preportion                   100
                                                         -----
                                                         58402
Ct. by Henry Peyton for ₺ 9: 2:11      1359
    by Thos. Young                      273              1632
                                                         -----
                                                         56770
To 6 p. Ct. for Collecting 56770 lbs. Tobo.              3414
                                                         -----
                                                         60184
Orderd. that the Collectors receive from Each
    tythable Person Fifty Six Pounds of tobo.            60480
         fraction in the Churchwd. hands                  296
         Do. Mistake in Do. hands                         100
                                                         -----
                                                          396
Cash Dr. Mr. Butler for a Chist & Repairing one
    pue                                                ₺ 1: 1: 6
            To Wm. Bennett for Horsblock & Steps         1: 0: 0
            To Mr. Cuthbert Harrison                      0: 5: 0
            To Mr. Henry Peyton for Tobo.                9: 2:11
                                                       ---------
                                                        11: 9: 5
Carsh Ct. by Mr. Robt. Wickliff                        ₺ 2:11: 2
          by Mr. Lewis Reno                              2:01: 7
          by Mr. James Scott                            6:16: 8
                                                       ---------
                                                        11: 9: 5
```

[33] Ordered that Mr. Lewis Reno be Continued Churchwd.

Ordered that Wm. Tebbs be Churchwrd. in the Room of Mr. Robt. Wickliff.

Orderd. that Lewis Reno be Collector of the Parrish Leavy givin bond and Security.

Orderd. that Thos. Machen be Clerk at Quantico Church in the Room of John Peyton and Attend Every Sunday.

Orderd. that Joseph Thurman be Continued Clerk at Broad run and Attend Every Sunday.

Orderd. that Catharin Bristor be Sexton in the Room of her husband Thos. Bristor decd.

Orderd. that John Carr be Continued Sexton at Quantico Church.

Orderd. that the Churchwardens advertise the Building two Churches in this Parish the walls to be of Stone or brick to be Each in the Clear not above Sixty foot long and thirty foot wide, for workmen to bring in Planes on Easter Tuesday Next if fair, and if not, the Next fair day.

Orderd. that Mr. Henry Peyton be vestryman in the Room of Isaac
Farguson removed.

Orderd. that Mr. Foushe Tebbs be Vestryman in the Room of John
Baxter removed.

[34 blank, 35] At a Vestrey held at Quantico Vestrery house for
the Parish of Ditigen the 24th Day of July 1752

Present: Mr. James Scott, Minister; Mr. Lewis Reno, Mr. Wm. Tibbs,
Churchwardens; Richard Blackburn, Benja. Grason, John Deskins,
Anthony Seale, Bertd. Ewell, Robt. Wickliff, James Nisbitt, Henry
Peyton, Feeushee Tebbs, Vestreymen:

Ordered the Tobacco Leavd. for Building the Churches be Netted
and made Croop & sold by the Churchwardens to the highest bider for
cash at Prince Wm. Court house at Next Court and the Money to be lett
out to Interest they takeing bond and security of the Persons that
takes the same.

Ordered that as Mr. Richards to whome our Churches ware Lett Last
Vestrey has refused to Give security according to that Vestreys
Orders it is therefore now Ordered that the Churchwardens again
Advertise in the Virgina. Gazts. & Other Publick Places that
Undertakers may Meet to agree with this Vestrey on the first Monday in
Octobr. Next being the secd. of that Month to Agree for two Churches
as before Mentioned & the Undertaker to give security at the time of
undertaking the same.

Ordered that Revd. James Scott, Thos. Harrison, Lewis Reno, John
Diskins, Anhony. Seale, Henry Peyton, Wm. Tibbs or anney foure of them
are to Vew the most Convient Place to Build the uper Church on &
Report the same to the Next Vestrey.

[36] At a Vestrey held at Quantico Vestrey house for the Parish
of Ditingen on the secd. Day of Oct. 1752

Prest.: Mr. James Scott, Minr.; Mr. Wm. Tibbs, Lewis Reno,
Chwds.; Thos. Harrison, John Diskins, Anta. Seale, James Nisbet,
Henry Peyton, Fushe Tebbs, Capt. Batrand Ewel & Colo. Ricd. Blackburn,
Vestrey men:

Ordered that half the Cash in the hands of the Church wardens be
paid by them to William More & Gabrel Muffett or there Order On
demand who have this Day enter'd into bond & Articles to buld a brick
Church in the uper part of this Parish for which said Cash they are to
allow ten Thousand pounds of tobacco & they are to have ninty
thousand pound of Tobacco for Building the said Church.

Ordered that the Church Wardens & the Revd. James Scott Take Bond
& Security of Wm. Wyat for the Building a stone Church in the town of
Dumfries for which he is to have Eighty Thousand pounds of Cropp
Tobacco & After Bond & Security Given the Churchwardens are to Pay to
the said Wyat the Other half of the Cash in their hands & he the said
Wiat is to Disct. ten thousd. pounds of tobacco for the same.

Ordered that the articles & Plans be Lodged by the Church wardens
in the hands of the Revd. James Scott.

[37] At a Vestrey held at Quantico Vestrey house for the Parish
of Ditingen the 30 Day of Octr. 1752

Prest.: Mr. James Scott, Ministr.; Mr. Wm. Tibbs & Lewis Reno, Cwds.; Thos. Harrison, John Deskens, Antho. Seale, James Nisbet, Henry Peyton, Fushe Tibbs, Capt. Battrand Ewel, Colo. Ricd. Blackburn, Vestrey men:

DITINGEN PARISH	Dr.
To the Revd. James Scott Minsr.	16000
To the Do. for 4 pr. Ct. to make it neat	640
To Do. for Cask	640
To Thos. Mitchem Reader at Quantico	1200
To Joseph Thurman Reader at Broad run	1200
To John Carr Sexton at Quantico	600
To Cathrine Bristo Sexton at Broad Run	600
To Burr Harrison Clk. Vest.	500
To Do. for the Prosesioners Reports & Orders & Recording the same	400
To Capt. Batrand Ewel for keeping a Blind man	800
To Nicholas Snow a pore man	530
To Peter Wagener for Coping the List of tithables & for Other sundry Artickles	362
To Wm. Benett fror keeping a blind man	800
To Benjaman Parker for keeping his Brother Ricd.	600
To John Crump for Returning two rits	16
To Samuel Stone one Levy Over Chargd.	57
To Doctrs. Fee for cureing Elias Ward if the cure be Perfect	1500
[38] To Do. for cureing John Dilgarn	750
To Doctr. James Nisbet for Meddisons	113
To the Revd. James Scott pr. Acct. 7:16: 6 at	1252
To Mr. Robt. Wickliff nursing Thos. More	120
To Youngs Exrs. pr. acct.	32
To Richd. Kinner for buring Joseph Estep & Other Accts.	480
To Mr. James Scott for the gleab	12000
To Colo. Ricd. Blackburn & Colo. Thos. Harrison to there Part of a Lawers fee at the suit of Peyton	266
To Gabrel Murphey for Boarding Sarah Shadburn	400
To Wm. More and Gabrel Muffitt towds. Bulding the Church at Readmans	22101
To Wm. Wyat for Building the Church at Quantico	19500
	83459
By Ct.	606
	82853
To 6 pr. Ct. for Collecting	4971
	87824
Ct. By 1155 Tithable person @ 76	87780

Due the Collectrs. 44

By Mr. Seale by an Old Fraction	245
By Mr. Wickliff by Do.	64
By Lewis Reno by Do.	297
	606

Ordered that the Collecttors receive of Each Tithable Person Seventy Six Pounds of Tobaco.

Ordered that Mr. Wm. Tibbs & Colo. Ricd. Blackburn be Churchwds. they giving Bond & Security.

[39] Ordered that Thos. Mitchem be Continued Clerk at Quantico.

Ordered that Joseph Thurman be Contd. Clerk at Broad run.

Ordered that John Carr be Contd. Sexto. at Quantico.

Ordered that Cathrine bristoe be Contd. Sexton at Broad run.

Ordered that Colo. Blackburn, Capt. Battrand Ewel, Colo. Thos. Harrison & Mr. Deskins Vew the Gleeb Buildings.

Ordered that Quantico Church be Built as Nigh the Old Church as Conveanently can on the Back Side.

At a Vestrey held at Quantico Vestrey house for the Parish of Ditingen this 5th Day of Aprill 1752

Prest.: Mr. Wm. Tibbs & Colo. Ricd. Blackburn, Cwd.; Mr. Robt. Wickliff, Colo. Benjaman Grason, Mr. Anthony Seale, Mr. Lewis Reno, Mr. John Deskens, Mr. Henry Peyton, Vestreyman:

On Examining the Returns of the Processioners And finding them Elegal and not Accdg. to Law it is Ordered that they be not Registered.

Ordered that Wm. Tibb be Collector for the Ensuing Yeare.

[40 blank, 41] At A Vestrey Held a Quontico Vestrey House in Ditingen Parish Decr. the 20th 1753

Present: Revd. James Scott, Minister; Colo. Ricd. Blackburn, Mr. Wm. Tibbs, Mr. John Deskins, Colo. Benjaman Grason, Mr. James Nisbet, Mr. Fushey Tibbs, Lewis Reno, Mr. Anthony Seale, Majr. Batrd. Ewel, Mr. Henry Peyton, Vestreymen:

DITINGIN PARISH

	Dr.
To the Revd. James Scoot Minsr.	16000
To Do. for Casq	640
To Do. 4 pr. Ct. for Makeing it Neat	640
To Mr. Thos. Mitcham Reader At Quantico	1200
To Joseph Thurman Reader at Broad Run	1200
To John Carr Sexton at Quantico	600
To Wd. Bristo Sexton at Broad Run	600
To Burr Harrison Clk. Vestrey	500
To Doct. Nisbets Acct.	3218
To John Anderson for Bording John Larny an Orphan	800
To Mr. John Graham Clk. Acct.	297
To Mildren Douncon for Makeing Surpilas	250
To Phillo. Wayters for keeping Gillen Morcanry a pre. Child	534
To Wm. Copia one Levi over Charged	76
To Colo. Ricd. Blackburn Chwd. Acct.	1675
To Arthor Bland for tending & Buring John Pasons	500
To Rebeck. Tomblin for Buring Bri. Conner	400
To Charles Wels one Levi overchargd.	76
[42] To Mr. John Peils for Keeping Blind Dick	600

```
To Benjaman Parker for keeping Ricd. Parker                         600
To Wm. Wiat for and towd. Building Quontico Church                18750
To 6 pr. Ct. for makeing it Neat & Prising                         1125
To Do. for Makeing his tobacco Croop Last Year                      475
To Wm. More & Gabrel Muffett for Building the Church
   at Redmons                                                     20000
To 6 pr. Ct. to Make the same Croop                                1200
To John Carr for keeping John Fooster one Month                     100
To John Barker for two Levies over paid                             152
To Silvester Monrony a pore Man                                     400
To George Britt for keeping a pore Man                              200
To 6 pr. Ct. for collecting 72208                                  4332
To the fraction in the Churchwardens hands                          317
                                                                  77457
                            CONTRA                                  CT.
By Richard Jarvice for Mary Sewel 20/ and                           520
By Mr. Henry Peyton Gent. for Phill. Spiller                        493
By John Diskins for Ballance                                        466
By Wm. Tibbs for Do.                                                216
                                                                   1695
By 1242 Tithable Persons at 61 pr. pole                           75762
                                                                  77457
```

Ordered that the Collectors Receive from Each Tyhable Person
the sum of Sixty one pounds of Tobacco it being the next parish Leavy
for this Yeare prest.

Ordered that Colo. Richd. Black Burn & Mr. John Deskins be Church
Wardens for the prest. Year.

[43] Ordered that Colo. Richard Blackburn Gent. be parish
Collector for the Present Yeare & that he gives bond with Security
for the paymt. of the severall Claims.

Ordered the Clerks of Each Church be Continued for the Ensuing
Yeare.

Ordered Colo. Benjamin Grason, Colo. Thomo. Harrison, James
Nisbett, Henry Peyton, & Wm. Tibbs or any three of them Vew the
gleeb Buildings & Receive them if found Sufficient.

Ordered that the Church Wardens bind Sarah Sewel a Malatto
Baseborn Child to Richd. Jarvice Accord. to Law.

Ordered the Church wardens bind Gillian Morean a Base Borne
Child to Philomon Wayters Senr. According to Law.

[44 blank, 45] At a Vestrey held at Quantico Vestreyhouse the
23d day of Decr. 1754

Present: Mr. James Scott, Minister; Mr. John Deskin Chwd.; Mr.
Robt. Wickliff, Collo. Benja. Grayson, Mr. Wm. Tibbs, Mr. Foushee
Tebbs, Mr. Lewis Reno, Mr. Antho. Seale, Mr. James Nesbett, Mr.
Hen. Peyton, Majr. Betrand Ewell, Vest. Men:

DETTINGEN PARISH

                                                                    Dr.

```
To the Revd. James Scott Ministr.                                 16000
To Do. for Cask                                                     640
```

To Do. for 4 p. Cent to Make it Neet	640
To Mr. Thos. Mitchum Reader at Quantico	1200
To Mr. Joseph Thurman Reader at Broad Run	1200
To John Carr Sexton at Quantico	600
To Cathron Bristo Sexton at Broad Run	600
To Burr Harrison Clk. of the Vestrey	500
To Mr. Wm. Tebbs for work done at the Chapple	75
To Mr. Abraham Farrow 7 Parish Leavies Over Chd.	427
To Robt. Sinkler for Work done at the Chapple	45
To Mr. Wm. Waite for & toward Building Quantico Church	18750
To 6 p. Ct. for Makeing it Crop & Prising	1125
To Wm. Moore & Gabril Muffitt for & Toward Building the Church at Redmons	20000
To 6 pr. Ct. for Making it Crop	1200
To Wm. Seale Sheriff Acct.	52
[46] To Mr. Sebastine to be Left in Churchwardens Hands till he brings in his Acct.	1000
To John Carr for Keeping John Foster 2 months	200
To Mr. John Graham Clk. as pr. Acct.	404
To James Nesbett as pr. Acct.	2582
To Collo. Richd. Blackburn L 3/10/6 @ 10/	705
To Rosanah Parker for Keeping Richd. Parker	600
To Phillamon Watters in balance for Keeping base born child the issue...	265
To James Johnston for Buring Wm. Turner	400
To Mary Scott for Keeping Cathron Posey	400
To Mr. John Diskin for Ellements for Broadrun Chaple	800
To Majr. Bertrand Ewell for Keeping Blind Dick	600
To Do. for Keeping Old Will	600
	71570
To 6 pr. Ct. for Collecting 71200 lbs. Tobo.	4272
	75842
By Credit Deducted	370
	75472
By 1307 Thyables @ 68 pr. Pole	75806
Fract.	334
[47]　　CONTRA	Cr.
By Capt. John Baylis	870

Ordered that Mr. John Deskins be Parish Collector the Present Yeare Giving bond & Security.

Ordered that Each Tythable Person Pay the Collector Fifty Eight Pounds of Tobacco.

Resolved that Majr. Bertrand Ewell be Churchwarden In the Roome of Collo. Richd. Blackburn he having Taken the Oath.

Ordered that the Clerks of Each Church be Continued For the Ensuing Yeare.

Ordered that five Hundred Pounds of Tobacco be paid to Silvester
Meroney at the Laying Next Parish Leavie if he is no Charge to ye
Parish from this time Untill then.

Ordered that the Churchwardens take Care of the Pore As Usuall.

[Signed] James Scott, Min., John Diskin, Cw.; Bertrand Ewell,
Antho. Seale, Thos. Harrison, H. Peyton, Wm. Tebbs, Benja. Grayson,
Lewis Reno, Robt. Wickliff, Foushee Tebbs, James Nesbitt.

[48 illegible, 49] At a Vestrey Held at Quantico Vestrey house
the 7th day of July 1755

Present: Mr. James Scott, Minr., Mr. John Diskin, Mr. Bertrand
Ewell Chuwds.; Mr. Antho. Seale, Mr. Lewis Reno, Mr. James Nisbett &
Mr. Foushee Tibbs, Collo. Richd. Blackburn, Vestrey Men:

Resolved that the Undertaker have Liberty to Agree with any Person
or Persons to build a Gallery at the Lower End of the Church the
Pavings into the Said Gallery to be without the Church & the
Property of the said Gallary to be Vested in the Persons Concerned
in the Building Thereof.

Ordered that Wm. Wyat have an Aditional Sum of Fourteen
Thous. Pounds of Croop Tobacco for...doors with glass over them &
Plain Neet Cutt Windows in the Church Now Building at Quantico which
said Tobacco is to be Levyed after the Said Church is Finished.

[50 blank, 51] At a Vestry held at Detingin Glbe. Decr. 8th
1755

Present: Mr. James Scott, Minister, Mr. John Deskin, Majr.
Batrand Ewel, Chwd.; Col. Thos. Harrison, Colo. Benj. Grason, Capt.
Antony Seal, Mr. Lewis Reno, Capt. Henry Peyton, Mr. Robt. Wickliff,
Mr. James Nisbet, Capt. Foushe Tibbs, Vestrey Men:

DITTINGIN PARISH

	Dr.
To the Revd. Mr. James Scott	16000
To Do. For Cask	640
To Do. 4 pr. Ct. to make it Neat	640
To Mr. Thos. Mitchum Reader at Quantico	1200
To Joseph Thurman Reader at Broad Run	1200
To Mr. Wm. Carr Sexton at Quantico	600
To John Wilo Sexton at Broad Run	600
To Burr Harrison Clerk of the Vestrey	500
To Mr. Wm. Wait For and towards Building Quantico Church	18750
To 6 pr. Ct. to Make it Crop	1125
To Mr. Wm. More & Gabriel Muffett For & Towards Building a Church at Redmans	20000
To 6 pr. Ct. to make it crop	1200
To Mr. John Graham Clks. Acct.	224
To John Bland Junr. to Levies Over Charg'd	150
To Thos. Snow a Pore man	530
To Robt. Linsey a Levey Overcharged	58
To Moses Bland for Buring Sarah Smith	300
To Rosanah Parker for Buring Richd. Parker	300

-20-

[52] To Mary Scott for keeping Cathrine Posey   1000
To George Latham for keeping a Child 6 weeks   200
To Wm. Miles for keeping a Child 6 weeks   200
To Adam Raines a Pore Man   530
To Wm. Carr for keeping Wm. Arington   800
Do. pr. Acct. ☩ 4:18: 6
               3: 5: 7   paid pr. Jno. Deskin
        Due   1:12:10 1/2 @ 12/6 pr. Hundred   263
To Doctr. James Nisbit pr. Acct.   2000
To Majr. Batrand Ewel for keeping Blind Dick   800
To Mr. John Deskins pr. Acct.   1000
To James Calk for Silvester Meroney a pore man   600
To Robert Hedges for keeping John Lawn   150
To Samuel Stone for keeping & burying Swinbury Plain   450
To Samuel Jackson for burying John Butler   300
                                                            72310
To 6 pr. Ct. for collecting 72310 lbs. of Tobacco   4338
                                                            76648

    Dr.   Ct.
By 1277 Tithable Persons @ 60 pr. Pole   76620
By Fraction Due from the Parish to the Collector   28
                                                            76648

        Order'd Each Tithable Person pay the Collector Sixty Pounds of
Tobacco being the Parish Leve for the Prest. Year.
        Order'd Majr. Bartrand Ewell & Mr. Lewis Reno be Church wardens
for the Ensuing Year.
        Order'd & Resolved that Patrick Hamrick Senr. be Free from Paying
his Parish Leavie for the time to come.
        Resolv'd that Matthew Moss, Warington Spiller, Richd. Gibson,
George Cowell, Samuel Stone Jnr. & Jno. Haley be free from Paying
their Parish Leave from the time to come.
        [53] Resolved that the Tobaco Leved for and towards Quantico and
Slaty Run Churches not to be Paid the several undertakers till furter
Orders of Vestry.
        Resolved that George Latham have 800 lbs. Tobo. at the Laying the
Next Parish Leave for keeping James Hazelridge an infant.
        Resolved that Wm. Mills have 800 lbs. of Tobacco Levied at Laying
the next Parish Levie for keeping Maryann Hazelrigg an infant.
        Resolv'd that Warington Spiller have 1000 lbs. of Tobo. Levied
at Laying the Next Levie for keeping Ann Davice an Infant.
        Order'd that Lewis Reno Collect the Parish Leavie for the Insuing
Year. Thos. Harrison, Benjaman Grason & Henry Peyton have agreed to
be his security for the Preformce. of the same & that they give Bond
to the Clk. of the Vestry.

[54 blank, 55] At a Vestrey held at Quantico Vestrey house August the
Twenty eighth Day 1756
        Present: Mr. James Scott, Minister; Bertrand Ewell, Lewis Renno,
Chw.; Thos. Harrison, Benja. Grayson, Richd. Blackburn, Wm. Tibbs,
Henry Peyton, James Nisbett, Robt. Wickliff, Foushee Tibbs:

Ordered that the Church at Quantico Built by Wm. Waite be Received he finding a Lock, Leads, Pulleys and Lines and Frames with the Creed.

Order'd that Mr. Lewis Reno, Pay the Tobacco now Levied in his hands to Mr. Waite or his Order Upon Demand.

Order'd that Lewis Reno Pay Gabril Murphey & Wm. More Undertakers of the Church at Redmons the Tobacco Levyed in his hands.

Order'd that Hugh Eady, Martin Harding and Benja. Rush or Any two of Them View the Gleeb buildings and Report to the Vestrey at the Laying the Next Levy.

Order'd that Mr. John Grayham have the Old Church he having Leave to Move it When he Pleases for Fifteen Hundred Pound of Tobacco.

Order'd that Mr. John Graham Move the Old Church before the Tenth day of October.

[56] Thomas Harrison, James Nisbett And Henry Peyton, Lewis Reno and Benja. Grayson decents to the Order of Receiving the Church at Quantico built by Mr. Wm. Waite for Reasons that it is not Finished According to the Said Writs, Articles with the Church Wardens and Farther that the Said Rev. James Scott has no Casting Vote in Receiving the said Church.

[57] At a Vestrey held at Dumfriss december the 21st Day 1756
Present: Mr. James Scott, Minister; Lewis Reno and Bertrand Ewell, Chwd.; Collo. Benja. Grayson, James Nisbett, Foushee Tibbs, Robt. Witcliff, Vestreymen:

DETENGEN PARISH

	Dr. lb.
To the Reverend James Scott Minister	16000
To Do. for Cask	640
To Do. 4 pr. Cent to make it Neat	640
To Mr. Thomas Mitchum Reader at Quantico	1200
To Joseph Thurman Reader at Broad Run	1200
To William Carr Sexton at Quantico	600
To John Willow Sexton at Broad Run	600
To Burr Harrison Clerk of the Vestry	500
To Mr. James Douglas As pr. Acct.	264
To Seale and Seale as pr. Acct.	120
To George Leathem for Keeping James Hazelrig	940
To William Mills for keeping Maryan Hazelrig	940
To Ledias Spiller for keeping and Do.	1000
To Wm. Bennett for keeping Duncan McDanil 2 years	1600
To Burr Harrison for Curing Adam Rains	400
To Do. for 7 Barrel Corn 50 lb. Tobacco	50
To Anastasious Rains a Pore Woman	530
To Richd. Rixey for keeping Francis Carpenter	184
[58] To Wm. Mills for Do.	174
To Mary Scott for keeping and Burying Catheron Posey	475
To Thomas Snow a pore man	530
To John Murray for Making a Chain and Fetters	150

```
To Clem Sere for buring Thos. Clerk                           200
To Joseph Butler for Making three horse blocks
    @ 200 lbs.                                                 600
To John Grayham for 2 Copys List Tythables                      32
To John Diskin for Correction last yeare                       343
To Wm. Rush and Mr. Harding for Viewing the gleeb
    buildings @ 100 lbs. each                                  200
To James Nisbitt as pr. Acct.                                  900
To Silvester Merroney a Pore man                               300
To Samuel Scurrey a Pore man                                   300
To Rachel Spiller for Keeping Blind Wm.                        585
To Thos. Dowell for Keeping old Wm.                            267
To Lewis Renno as pr. Acct.                                    727
To Wm. Carr as p. Acct.                                        605
To Collo. Bertrand Ewell for Keeping blind Dick                805
                                                             34674
To 6 pr. Cent for Collecting                                  2080
To George Brett for keeping Robt. Foster                       150
To Collo. Benja. Grayson payd Layer for his Opinion            172
                                                             37076
Cr. by 1268 Tythables at 30 lbs. Tobbacco pr. pole           38040
                                                               964
```

Order'd that Each Tythable person Pay the Collector 30 lbs. Tobcco.
Order'd that Mr. Lewis Reno and James Nisbitt be Church Wardens
the Ensuing Yeare and that they take Care of the poor as Usuall.
    [59] Order'd that Mr. John Grayham Pay unto Wm. Carr Fifteen
hundred Pounds of Tobacco for the old Church on his Giving Deeds for
two acres of Land where the New Church Stands if Required.   Bertrand
Ewell decents to the above order.
    Order'd that the Revered. James Scott Deliver the bonds and
Articles of Wm. Waite and More to Mr. James Nisbitt Churchwarden.
    Order'd that Lewis Reno be Collector the Ensuing yeare he
giving bond and Security to the Clerk of the Vestrey James Nisbett
Anthoney Seale his Security.

    [60 blank, 61] At a Vestrey held at Dumfries the 14th day of March
Called by the Church wardens to Consider what is Necessary to be done
in Relation to the Church built by Mr. Waite at Quantico and also the
Gleeb built by the Reverend James Scott
    Present: Mr. James Scott, Minstr.; Mr. James Nisbett, Mr. Lewis
Reno, Churchwds.; Mr. Benja. Grayson, Mr. Thos. Harrison, Mr. Foushee
Tibbs, Mr. Antho. Seale, Mr. Henry Peyton, Robt. Wickliff, Wm. Tibbs,
Vestmen.:
    Ordred. that the Churchwardens bring Suite against Mr. Wm. Waite
and his Securiteys for not Compleating the Church built by him at
Quantico according to his articles.
    Ordred. that the Churchwardens bring Suite against the Reverend
James Scott and his Securiteys for not Compleating the Gleeb building
according to his Articles.

    [62] At a Vestry held at Quantico Church the 8th day of October
1757
    Present: The Revd. James Scott, Minister; Henry Lee, Lewis Reno,

John Baylis, Foushee Tebbs, William Bennitt, William Seale, Thomas Harrison, John Buchanan, Vestrymen:

Henry Lee & Lewis Reno are Appointed Churchwardens of this Parish for this Present Year they having taken the oath prescribed by Law.

Burr Harrison is Appointed Clerk of this Vestry being first Sworn as Such.

On the Motion of William More he has Liberty to build a Gallary in the New Church near Cedar run in this parish and the Vestry have the Preferrence in Purchasing the Same when finished.

Signed: James Scott, Minister; Henry Lee, Lewis Reno, Chwdns.; Thos. Harrison, Wm. Seale, Jno. Buchanan, John Baylis, Willm. Bennitt, Foushee Tebbs.

[63] At a Vestry held in Dettingen Parish at Dumfries the 9th day of December 1757

Present: The Revd. James Scott, Minister; Henry Lee & Lewis Reno, Churchwardens; Henry Peyton, John Baylis, Foushee Tebbs, William Bennitt, Thomas Harrison, Wm. Carr, Wm. Seale, John Buchanan and John Hooe, Vestrymen:

DETTINGEN PARISH

	Dr. lbs. tobo.
To the Revd. James Scott Minister	16000
To Ditto for Cask	640
To Ditto 4 p. Ct. to make it Net	640
To Thos. Machen reader at Quantico	1200
To Joseph Thurman Reader at Broad Run	1200
To William Carr Sexton at Quantico	600
To John Willow Sexton at Broadrun	600
To Burr Harrison Clk. of the Vestry	500
To John Graham for Clks. fees	32
To Edward Hall for Burying Jean Crouch	400
To Elizabeth Patterson for keeping Mary Weedup 5 months	250
To Silvester Merony for rent	400
To Elizabeth Gwinn for keeping Richd. Jones 12 months	800
To Samuel Scurry a poor man	300
To Robert Hedges for keeping John Lawn two months and burying him	650
To Sarah Harris...Calvert for burying Griffith Watkins	300
To John Holliday for burying Elizabeth Parsons	400
To John Farrow for keeping and Nursing Alice Bowin a bastard Child	1000
[64] To William Walker for keeping Elizabeth Giles a Deaf and Dumb Orphan	829
To William Bennit for keeping and Burrying Duncan McDonald a poor man	800
To George Latham for keeping James Hazelrigg a poor Orphan	850

To William Mills for keeping Mary Ann Hazelrigg a poor Orphan   850
To Rachel Spiller for keeping and nursing Francis Carpenter   932
To Doctor James Nisbett p. Accot.   120
To Thomas Snow a poor man   530
To Messrs. Macrae & Douglas p. Accot.   171
To Isaac Kent a poor man   530
To Biddy Scails a poor Woman   300
To James Scott Clk. p. Accot.   512
To Lewis Reno Chwdn. for finding cloths for Silvester Merony   500
To William Carr p. accot.   366
To William Waite p. a former order of Vestry p. Agreement   14000
To Ditto for a plaister Cornice   3000
To be lodged in the hands of the Chwdns. in part for
   building a vestry house   1000
To 6 p. Ct. for Collecting 51202   3072
                                                                 ‾‾‾‾‾
                                                                 54274
To a fraction in Collectrs. hands   35
                                                                 ‾‾‾‾‾
                                                                 54309
                                                                   Cr.
By 1263 Tithables @ 43 lbs. p. pol.   54309

    Ordered the Churchwardens receive of Each Tithable person in his
Parish forty three pounds of Tobacco and pay the Same to the Several
parish Creditors.
    [65] Lewis Reno is appointed Collector of the Parish Levy this
present Year giving Bond and Security for his faithful performance.
    Ordered that the Seventeen thousand pounds of Tobacco levied for
William Waite be Lodged in the hands of the Churchwardens untill the
said Waite Compleat the Work Mentioned in a former order of Vestry.
    Ordered that the Churchwardens agree with Workmen to build a
Vestry house Sixteen feet Square near Majr. John Baylis's ordinary
the said John Baylis agreeing to give Land for the same.
    Thomas Machen is appointed Clerk of this Vestry and ordered that the
former Clerk deliver him the Records & papers belonging to the parish.
    Ordered the former Churchwardens deliver to the present the
articles Bonds etc. Concerning the parish work.
    [Signed] James Scott, Minister; Henry Lee, Lewis Reno,
Churchwardens; John Baylis, Foushee Tebbs, William Bennitt, John
Buchanan, John Hooe, Wm. Seale, William Carr, Henry Peyton.

    [66] At a Vestry Summoned and held at Quantico church the 12th of
April 1758 for Dettingen Parish
    Present: Henry Lee & Lewis Reno, Churchwardens; The Revd. James
Scott, Minister; Henry Peyton, Thomas Harrison, Foushee Tebbs, William
Bennitt, William Seale, John Hooe & John Buchanan, Vestrymen:
    Howson Hooe Gent. was sworn a Vestryman for this Parish and took
his Seat Accordingly.
    Present: Howson Hooe.
    Ordered the Churchwardens agree with a workman to make a table and
Benches for the Vestry house that is to be built by a former order of

Vestry.

Ordered that Colo. Henry Lee have Liberty to Cut the Hanging Post in the Gallary Putting a Pillar under the same gallary.

Signed: James Scott, Minister; Henry Lee, Lewis Reno, Churchwardens; Henry Peyton, William Seale, Thos. Harrison, Howson Hooe, Foushee Tebbs, John Buchanan, John Hooe, William Bennitt.

[67] At a Vestry Summoned and held for Dettingen Parish at Quantico Church the 29th of July 1758

Present: Henry Lee & Lewis Reno, Churchwardens; the Revd. James Scott, Minister; John Baylis, Howson Hooe, John Buchanan, Foushee Tebbs, William Carr, William Seale, John Hooe, Vestrymen:

Whereas there is a Difficiency in the work performed by Mr. William Waite in not putting Leads and Pullys in the Church windows built by him at Quantico and the Vestry being Convinced that the said Church has been Legally Received

Ordered the Churchwardens pay to the said William Waite Seventeen thousand pounds of Transferr Tobacco which is in their hands & Levied at the Laying the Last parish Levy upon an Additional agreement with him made, fourteen thousand whereof was ordered Crop, the said Deduction being made on account of the Said Difficiencys.

Resolved that the Churchwardens Advertise a Vestry house to be built at Colo. John Baylis's at the Fork of the roads where he now lives, Sixteen foot square, framed work, plank't above and below, one Pannel door, one Sash Window, with a Table & Convenient benches, one wooden outside Chimney, the said house to be Covered and Sealed with good Clap boards.

Signed: James Scott, Minster; Henry Lee, Lewis Reno, Churchwardens; John Baylis, Foushee Tebbs, Howson Hooe, Wm. Seale, John Hooe, John Buchanan, Will. Bennitt, Wm. Carr.

[68] At a Vestry Summoned and held for Dettingen Parish on Monday the 11th of December 1758 for Laying the Levy

Present: Lewis Reno, Churchwarden; John Baylis, Howson Hooe, William Carr, Foushee Tebbs, William Bennitt, William Seale, John Buchannan, Vestrymen:

DETTINGEN PARISH

	Dr. lbs. tobo.
To the Revd. James Scott Minister	16000
To Ditto for cask	640
To Ditto 4 p. Ct. to make it Net	640
To Thomas Machen Reader at Quantico	1200
To Ditto as Clerk of this Vestry	500
To Joseph Thurman reader at Ceader Run	1200
To John Willow Sexton at Ditto	600
To William Carr sexton at Quantico	600
To John Graham Clerk for Lists	32
To Silvester Meroney a poor man	800
To Samuel Scurry a poor man	530
To Wm. Walker for boarding and cloathing a Deaf and Dumb Child	400

```
To Thomas Snow a poor man                                          600
To James Gwinn for keeping Richd. Jones a blind Man                750
To John Griffin for Nursing a poor Child 2 years                  1000
                                                                  26292
Present:  Henry Peyton
To Mary Kent a poor Woman                                          500
To Rachel Spiller for keeping old Hester a poor Woman
an and Burying her                                                 500
Present:  Henry Lee, Churchwarden
To Capt. Wm. Carr for Margret Young                                500
To Colo. Henry Lee Chwdn. p. Accot.                                192
To be Lodged in the Chwdns. hands for Curing a
    deaf and dumb girl of a scald head when performed              400
[69] To Henry Floyd for keeping Mary Weedup 6 months               300
To Thomas Bird one Levy Overcharged last year                       43
To Eliza. Patterson for keeping Mary Weedup 6 months               300
To Francis Purnell p. Accot.                                        40
To John McMillion one Levy Overcharged                              43
To John Calvert one Levy Overcharged                                43
To George Calvert Youngr. one Levy overcharged                      43
To Eliza. Anderson Widow three Levys overcharged                   129
To Simon Luttrell p. Accot. for Clearing Church yard               300
Present:  Thomas Harrison
To Thomas Redman for Clearing Cedar run Churchyard                1200
To George Carter for horse blocks & Racks at Do. Church            865
To John Willow for Putting up a Dial post at Ditto                  50
To Capt. William Carr p. Accot.                                    453
Present:  The Revd. James Scott, Minister
To Doctr. James Nisbett former Chwdn. p. Accot.                    420
To the Revd. James Scott p. Accot.                                 384
To John Murray p. Accot.                                           100
To William More p. Accot.                                          250
                                                                  33347
To 6 p. Ct. for Collecting 33347                                   1999
To Balla. in Collectors hands 400 lbs. Tobacco                    35346
                        CONTRA                                      CR.
By Lewis Reno Chwdn. Ballance p. Accot.                             18
By 1276 Tithables @ 28 lbs. p. pol.                               35728
                                                                  35746
```

Ordered the Churchwardens pay Daniel Stewart forty three pounds of
Tobacco for a Levy Overcharged him last year out of the Fraction in
their hands.

Ordered that Henry Lee and Lewis Reno the present Churchwdns. be
Continued as Such till laying the next parish Levy. Lewis Reno is
appointed Collector of the parish Levy giving Bond with Sufficient
Security to the Clerk.

Signed: James Scott, Minister; Henry Lee, Lewis Reno,
Churchwardens; Henry Peyton, Foushee Tebbs, John Baylis, Howson Hooe,
William Bennitt, Wm. Carr, Wm. Seale, Thos. Harrison, John Buchanan.

At a Vestry Summoned and held for Dettingen Parish the 15th day

of December 1759
    Present: The Revd, James Scott, Minister; Henry Lee & Lewis Reno,
Churchwardens; Henry Peyton, Foushee Tebbs, William Bennett, John
Hooe, John Baylis, Howson Hooe, William Carr, William Seale, John
Buchanan, Vestrymen:

DETTINGEN PARISH	Dr. lbs. tobo.
To the Reverend James Scott Minister	16000
To Ditto for Cask	640
To Ditto 4 p. Ct. to make it Net	640
To Thomas Machen reader at Quantico	1200
To George Carter reader at Cedar run	1200
To Thomas Machen Clk. Vestry and for Processioning Service	800
To John Willow Sexton	600
To Francis Purnell Sexton	600
To John Graham Clk. p. Accot.	32
[71] To Thomas Snow a poor man	600
To George Thayer for keeping blind Dick	200
To Capt. Carr for cloths for blind Dick	55
To Henry Floyd for keeping Mary Weedup a poor Woman	511
To Messrs. Macrae & Douglas p. Accot.	1000
To Mary Kent a poor Woman	500
To John Pierce a poor man	600
To Henry Cooper a poor man	400
To John Johnson a poor Man	530
To Aaron Drummond for supporting Eleanor Jones 4 months	200
To John Bland Junr. 2 Levies overpaid	56
To Mr. Archibald Henderson p. Accot.	289
To Mr. William Scott for 1 pr. hinges and fixing up Quantico Church door	50
To Colo. Henry Lee Chwdn. p. Accot. for the Church Elemts.	400
To the Revd. Mr. Scott p. Accot. for Ditto	400
To Elizabeth Metcalf for Nursing a bastard Child	800
To Lewis Reno Chwdn. p. Accot.	38
To 6 p. Ct. for Collecting 28241 Tobo.	1706
To fraction in Chwdns. hands	574
	30521
CONTRA	CR.
By 1327 Titha. at 23 lb. tobo. p. Pol.	30521

    Ordered that the Churchwardens Collect of Each Tithable person
in this parish the Sum of twenty three pounds of Tobacco and pay
the Same to the Several parish Creditors.
    Ordered that Lewis Reno and John Baylis Gent. be Churchwardens for
the Ensuing Year.
    Ordered that John Baylis gent. be Collector of the Parish Levy
the Ensuing Year, giving Bond to the Clerk.

Signed, James Scott, Ministr.; [72] Lewis Reno, John Baylis,
Churchwardens; Henry Peyton, Henry Lee, Foushee Tebbs, Wm. Bennett,
Howson Hooe, Wm. Carr, Wm. Seale, Jno. Buchanan.

At a Vestry Summoned and held for Dettingen Parish the 17th day
of September 1760
　　Present: Lewis Reno & John Baylis Chwdns.; Foushee Tebbs, William
Bennett, William Seale, John Buchanan & John Hooe, Vestrymen:
　　Resolved that the Vestry of this Parish meet at the Glebe the
day the parish Levy is next laid, in order to View the Buildings
thereon, whether performed According to the Articles entred into by
the Revd. Mr. James Scott the undertaker.
　　Signed, John Baylis, Lewis Reno, Churchwardens; Foushee Tebbs,
William Bennett, William Seale, John Buchanan, John Hooe.

　　[73] At a Vestry Summoned and held for Dettingen Parish the 15th
day of December 1760
　　Present: Lewis Reno & John Baylis, Chwdns.; The Revd. James
Scott, Minister; Henry Peyton, Henry Lee, William Bennett, William
Seale, Howson Hooe, John Hooe & John Buchanan, Vestrymen:

DETTINGEN PARISH		Dr. Tobo.
To the Revd. James Scott Minister		16000
To Ditto for Cask		640
To Ditto 4 p. Ct. to make it Net		640
To Thomas Machen Reader at Quantico		1200
To George Carter Reader at Cedar Run		1200
To John Dalton Sexton at Quantico		600
To John Willow Sexton at Cedar Run		600
To John Graham Clerk p. Accot.		32
To Benjamin Sebastian p. Accot.	⊹ 9:15: 1	
To Colo. John Baylis p. Accot.	1: 3: 5	
To Archibald Henderson p. Accot.	1:14: 0	
To Daniel Payne p. Accot.	0: 3: 6	
To Thomas Raimey for Carrying William Rhodes and his wife to Loudoun County, Cameron Parish		160
To Thomas Boggess for supporting Roger Walden a poor man		50
To Richard Robinson Junr. for digging Joseph Hides grave	0: 2: 6	
To Joseph Smith for making Dos. Coffin	0:10: 0	
To Burr Harrison for Attending and Burring John Cotter		600
Present: William Carr, Vestryman:		
To Peter Cornwell a poor man		500
[74] To Allan Macrae gent. for Wine for the Church	1: 4: 0	
To Philemon Waters for supporting Elizabeth Walker		500
To Simon Luttrell for keeping Martha McMillion 2 months		100
To Mason Bennett for keeping Ditto 2 Weeks		25
To John Peirce a poor man		600

-29-

To James Calk for Burrying Mary Kent a poor woman
  besides what her Estate was appraised to £ 0:12: 0
Present: Thomas Harrison, Vestryman:
To Bridget Scails a poor Woman   250
To James Grinstead for burrying & finding Thos.
  Mollahon   350
To John Johnson a poor man   750
To George Thayer for keeping Margaret Bryan and her
  Child three Weeks   75
To George Thayer for Cloaths and keeping Blind
  Dick p. account   £ 2: 1: 9   &   325
To the Revd. Mr. James Scott for Elements for Slaty
  Run church   3: 4: 0
To Obed Calvert one Levy Overcharged   23
To James Wilson one Levy Overcharged   23
To Thomas Snow a poor Man   600
To Rachel Spiller for keeping Mary Weedup a poor Woman   600
To George Ford for Burrying a poor Woman and keeping
  her Six Weeks   375
To George Brett Gent. for keeping a poor man one Month   50
To Joseph Smith for Part building the Vestryhouse
                                              0:14: 0   &   1000
To James Nisbett p. Accot. for keeping & Physicking
  George Steele   1195
To George Carter for Work at the upper Church   50
To William More for the Gallery   100: 0: 0
To John Gallahue one Levy Overcharged   23
[75] To William More for Extraordinary service
  in building Cedar Run Church   50:16: 8
To Ditto for 3 Pediments @ 40/ each   6: 0: 0
                                            £188: 0:11
To William Seale p. Accot.   120
To Doctor Nisbett for Attendance and Medecines to
  John Johnson a poor man   200
To tobacco Levied & to be sold to discharge Cash
  Debts   26865
                                                               56321
To 6 p. Ct. for Collecting 55747 Tobacco   3345
To a fraction in the Collectors hands   610
                                                               59776
                        CONTRA   CR.
By Lewis Reno Gent.   574
By 1287 Tithables @ 47 lb. Tobo. p. pol   59202
                                                               59776

     Ordered that the Churchwardens of this Parish receive of Each
Tithable person in the said parish the Sum of forty Seven pounds
of Tobacco and that they pay the same to the Severall parish
Creditors.
     Resolved that the Churchwardens of this Parish apply to the
Churchwardens of Overwharton parish in Stafford County to know

Whether they will Join them in building and Supporting a work house.
    Resolved that William More deliver to the Churchwardens the Gallary built by him in Cedar Run Church.
    Lewis Reno and John Baylis Gent. are Appointed Churchwardens for the Ensuing Year.
    Ordered by Consent of the Revd. James Scott undertaker of the Glebe work, And this Vestry, William Edie & Benjamin Tomkins are appointed to View the Glebe work performed by the said Revd. [76] Mr. Scott in this Parish and if they disagree in their opinions of the said work According to the Agreement Entered into by him that they Choose an Umpire and Assess what Damages they think the Parish hath Sustained, if they think the work insufficient, between this and the first of next March.
    Ordered that the Churchwardens of this parish pay John Willow one hundred pounds of Tobacco out of the Fraction in their hands.
    Ordered that James Nisbett who has the Bonds between this Parish and the Revd. James Scott about building the Glebehouses deliver the same to the Churchwardens who are ordered to Attend the Persons Appointed to view the said Work with the sd. Writings.
    Ordered the Churchwardens pay Thomas Machen Clerk of this Vestry five hundred pounds of Tobacco out of the Fraction in their hands.
    Signed, James Scott, Minister; John Baylis, Churchwardens; Henry Peyton, William Bennett, Henry Lee, John Hooe, John Buchanan, Thomas Harrison, William Seale, Howson Hooe, Vestrymen:

    [77] At a Vestry Summoned and held for Dettingen Parish the 4th day of January 1762
    Present: John Baylis and Lewis Reno, Churchwardens; the Revd. James Scott, Minister; Foushee Tebbs, William Bennett, John Buchanan, William Carr, Vestrymen:

	DETTINGEN PARISH	Dr. tobo.

	Dr. tobo.
To the Revd. James Scott Minister	16000
To Ditto for p. Ct. and cask	1280
To Thomas Machen Reader at Quantico	1200
To George Carter Reader at Slaty Run	1200
To John Dalton Sexton at Quantico	600
To John Willow Ditto at Slaty Run	600
To John Graham Clerk	32
To Peter Cornwell a poor man	500
To Mary Peirce a poor Woman	400
To George Thayer for keeping Blind Dick	800
To Bridget Scails a poor Woman	400
To John Johnston a poor man	1200
To Thomas Snow a poor man	600
To Moses Jeffries for keeping Mary Weedup	600
Present: Henry Peyton & William Seale, Vestrymen:	
To Darby Peirce for nursing Phebe Mitchell one year	1000
To John Summers for keeping Richd. Gibson 2 Weeks	50
To Phileman Waters for keeping Elizabeth Walker	500

To Elizabeth Gun for keeping Martha McMillion two
months   100
To Benjamin Brett for keeping Ditto 10 months   500
To Thomas Arrington for keeping Margt. Cornwell   600
To Richard Wright for keeping & nursing Jane Metcalf   400
To Susan Castor for keeping Mary Steele   400
[78] To Richard Johnston a poor man   120
To Margt. Bryan a poor Woman   500
To Capt. William Carr p. Accot.   482
To John Baylis p. Accot.   358
To the Rev. James Scott p. accot. ± 3: 4: 0 @ 10/p. Ct.   640
To Thomas Boggess for keeping & Burrying Roger Walden   500
To Leven Powell S.S. p. Accot.   144
To James Scott Clk. one Levy Overcharged   47
To Howson Hooe 1 Levy Overcharged   47
To George Carter for work on the upper Church   220
To William More p. Ditto Accot.   100
To John Willow Sexton a further Allowance   100
To Doctr. James Nisbett p. Accot.   3550
To Thos. Machen Clk. Vestry   500
To 6 p. Ct. for Collecting   2177
To fraction in Collectors hand   523
                                                              38970
                          CONTRA   CR.
By 1299 Tithables at 30 1b. p. pol   38970

    Foushee Tebbs is Appointed Parish Collector the Ensuing year And
ordered that each tithable person in the parish pay him thirty pounds
of Tobacco p. pol, and that he pay the same to the Several Parish
Creditors.
    Foushee Tebbs and William Bennett are appointed Churchwardens the
Ensuing year.
    Ordered that Lewis Reno Gent. pay to the present Churchwardens Eleven
pounds five Shillings and eight pence to be Applyed as the Vestry
thinks fit.
    [79] Resolved that William Ellzey Gent. be appointed Attorney for
the Parish, he have one third of the Fines Recovered, And ordered that
his Letter that binds him to this Agreement be lodged amongst the
Records of this Vestry.
    Ordered that the Damage Assessed by William Adie, William Tompkins
and William White of twenty pounds be paid to the Churchwardens of this
parish to be applied to and for the reparation of the Glebe houses, they
being the persons appointed and agreed on by order of the Last Vestry,
John Baylis Gent. dissents to the above order.
    Ordered the Churchwardens advertise the Letting the Repairs of the
Glebe houses.
    Signed, James Scott, Minister; Foushee Tebbs, William Bennett,
Churchwardens; John Buchannan, Henry Peyton, William Carr, Lewis Reno,
John Baylis, Wm. Seale, Vestrymen.

    At a Vestry summoned & held for Dettingen Parish the 17th day of

January 1763
    Present: Foushee Tebbs & William Bennett, Churchwardens; The
Revd. James Scott, Minister; Henry Peyton, Henry Lee, Lewis Reno, John
Baylis, Thomas Harrison, William Carr, Howson Hooe, John Hooe, & John
Buchanan, Vestrym.:

	DETTINGEN PARISH	Dr. tobo.
To the Revd. Mr. James Scott Minister		16000
To Ditto for p. Ct. & cask		1200
To Thomas Machen Reader at Quantico		1200
To Ditto as Clerk of this Vestry		500
To George Carter reader at Slaty Run		1200
To John Dalton Sexton at Quantico		600
To John Willow Sexton at Slaty Run		600
To John Graham Clk. p. Accot. for List of Tithables		35
To Peter Cornwell a poor man		500
To Mary Peirce a poor Woman		600
To John Johnson a poor man		1200
To George Thayer for keeping Blind Dick		800
To Thomas Snow a poor man		600
To Moses Jeffry's for keeping Mary Weedup		600
To Margaret Bryan a poor woman		750
To William Calvert 3 Parish Levys Overcharged		90
To Richard Gibson 1 Ditto Ditto		30
To George Calvert 1 Ditto Ditto		30
To Ann Farrow 1 Ditto Ditto		30
To William Bowling 1 Ditto Ditto		30
To James Battoe 1 Ditto Ditto		30
To Richard Robinson 1 Ditto Ditto		30
To William Crouch 1 Ditto Ditto		30
To John Diskin 4 Ditto Ditto		120
To Ditto 1 Ditto in 1760		47
To Capt. William Carr p. Accot. ⊥ 5: 5:11		
To Archibald Henderson p. Accot. 2: 6: 7 1/2		
To the Rev. Mr. Scott p. Accot. 3: 4: 0		
To Mr. Allan Macrae p. Accot. 1: 9: 4		
To Eliza. Gun for keeping Martha Whailey		600
To Phileman Waters for keeping & burying Elizabeth Walker		400
[81] To John Willow Sexton a further Allowance		100
To John Bland for keeping Richard Gibson		500
To Moses Jeffrey's for looking after Thos. Overall		1057
To Ditto for looking after Andrew Blair and boarding him 7 Months		400
To Mardun Van Eventon for work done on the Lower Church 3: 7: 0		
To William Oldham for Nursing a base born Child 5 months		430
To James Norris a poor man		530
To Robert Hamilton for keeping Ann Hamilton a blind Girl		500
To Tobacco levied to discharge Cash Account		2000

```
To Vallentine Higgs                                        500
To Catherine Smith a poor Woman                            400
To Thomas Lawson p. Accot. for Eliza. Corin    1: 9: 7
                                              ‾‾‾‾‾‾‾‾‾‾‾ ‾‾‾‾‾‾
                                             £ 17: 2: 5½  34349
To 6 p. Ct. for Collecting                                2069
To Lewis Oden for Elizabeth                                150
To a fraction                                              392
                                                         ‾‾‾‾‾‾
                                                          36960
                         CONTRA                           CR.

By 1232 Tithables @ 30 lb. p. pol                         36960
```

Foushee Tebbs Gent. is appointed Collector for the Parish the
Ensuing year and ordered that Each Tithable person in this parish pay
him thirty pounds of tobacco, and that he pay the Same to the Several
Parish Creditors.

Foushee Tebbs and William Bennett are appointed Churchwardens for
the Ensuing Year.

[82] Ordered the Churchwardens Sell the Tobacco Levied to discharge
Cash accots. against the parish for the best price they can get.

Ordered that Foushee Tebbs Churchwarden pay to Wm. Ellzey Eleven
pounds five Shillings towards discharging his Accot. Against the Parish.

Resolved that Cuthbert Bullett be Attorney for the Parish, William
Ellzey gent. having Resigned being the Same.

Ordered the Churchwardens Advertise the Letting the Repairs of the
Glebe houses.

Resolved that William Ellzey be a Vestryman in the Room of William
Seale who is removed out of the Parish.

Signed, James Scott, Minister; Foushee Tebbs, Wm. Bennett, Chwdns.;
William Carr, Henry Lee, Howson Hooe, Thomas Harrison, John Buchanan,
Lewis Reno, Henry Peyton, John Hooe, Vestrymen.

[83] At a Vestry held for Dettingen Parish the 28th day of November
1763

Present: the Revd. James Scott; William Bennett, Churchwarden; Lewis
Reno, John Baylis, William Ellzey, Henry Peyton, John Buchanan, Howson
Hooe, William Carr, John Hooe, & Thomas Harrison, Vestry Men:

```
                    DETTINGEN PARISH                   Dr. tobo.

To the Revd. James Scott Minister                      16000
To Ditto for Per Cent                                   1260
To Thomas Machen Reader at Quantico                     1260
To Ditto Clerk of Vestry & for Processioning Service    1000
To George Carter Reader At Slaty Run Church             1200
To John Dalton Sexton at Quantico                        600
To John Willow Sexton at Slaty Run                       600
To John Graham Clk. p. Accot.                             76
To Mary Splane for mending the Surplice at Quanto.        50
To Danl. Williams for keeping Mary Walkers child
   one year                                             1000
To Archibald Bigby p. Accot.                             125
```

```
To Bridget Scales a poor Woman                                              300
To William Crouch one Levy overpaid last year                                30
To James Foley one Ditto Overpaid in 1761                                    47
To Henry Floyd one Ditto Overpaid Last Year                                  30
To Thomas Anderson one Ditto overpaid last year                              30
To Doctr. James Nisbett p. Accot.                                          3080
To Henry Norman 2 Levys Overpaid last Year                                   60
To Phebe  Mitchell p. Accot.                                               1500
To keeping Blind Dick & to be left in Chwdns. hands
   & to be settled by them to the Claimers                                  800
To Allan Macrae p. Accot.          ⅃  1: 3: 4
To Elizabeth Gwinn for burying Blind Dick                                   125
[84] To Moses Jeffrys for keeping & nursing Sundrys as
   per Accot.                                                              2000
To John Summers for keeping Richard 2 Weeks & for
   3 1/2 yds. bro. linnen              0: 4: 4    &                           50
To John Willow for pinns for upper Church Windows                           100
To Alexander Parker for the Cure & care of John
   Richardson in part                                                       750
To Jacob Calvert p. Accot.                                                  150
To Archibald Henderson p. Accot.        0:17: 7
To Capt. William Carr p. Ditto          6:16: 9
To Stephen Pilcher for keeping Henry Gradey a Child                         800
To James Scott Clk. p. Acco.            3:12: 0
To Mrs. Wigginton for keeping a Child two years                            1500
To Doctor James Lawrie for Attendg. Geo. Thayer                            1000
To Margt. Barker for keeping Ann Chamblin                                   150
To Elizabeth Gunn for keeping Ditto                                          75
To John Willow as a further Allowance being Sexton                          100
To John Willow a poor man on Accot. of his wife                             300
To Ditto one Levy Overcharged last year                                      30
To Richard Coffer for taking of Elizabeth Corum                             100
To Peter Cornwell a poor man                                                500
To Mary Pierce a poor Woman                                                 400
To James Johnson for John Johnson      1: 5: 3    &                        1200
To Thomas Snow a poor man                                                   600
To George Carter p. Accot.                                                  125
To Margt. Bryan a poor Woman to be laid out by the
   Churchwardens                                                            500
To Mr. Wm. Grayson for levys overpaid in 1761                               376
To Robert Hamilton for keeping a blind Girl Ann Hamilton                    500
To James Norris a poor Man                                                  530
To Capt. William Ellzey p. Accot. ⅃ 10: 2: 6
[85]                              ⅃ 24:11: 9 1/2
To Tob. to Discharge Cash                                                  5000
                                                                          ─────
                                                                          46049
To 6 p.Ct. for Collecting 46049 lbs. tobo. is                              3760
                                                                          ─────
                                                                          49809
To a fraction in Collectors hands                                          1116
                                                                          ─────
                                                                          50925
```

By 1455 Tithables @ 35 lb. tobo. pr. pol   50925

Ordered that Howson Hooe and Lewis Reno Gent. be Churchwardens for the Ensuing Year.

Ordered that each tithable person in this parish pay the Sum of thirty five pounds of Tobacco to Lewis Reno Gent. he being parish Collector the Ensuing year, & it is also ordered that he Enter into bond for his faithfull performance with the Clk.

Ordered the Churchwardens Advertise the Repairs of the Glebe houses and Lett the same to the Lowest bidder.

Signed, James Scott, Minister; Howson Hooe, Lewis Reno, Churchwardens; William Bennett, Thomas Harrison, William Ellzey, John Buchanan, Foushee Tebbs, Vestrymen.

[86] At a vestrey Called and held for Dettengin parish the 19th day of Febry. 1764

Present: William Carr, John Buchanon, Churchwardens; Colo. Henry Lee, Lewis Reno, John Hooe, Howson Hooe, William Bennett, Vestreymen:

DETTENGIN PARISH		Dr.
To the Revd. Mr. James Scott Clk.		16000
To Ditto for pr. Ct. and Cask		1280
To George Carter Reader at Slatey Run		1200
To John Reno Clk. vestrey		500
To John Dalton Sexton Quantico		600
To John Wellow Sixton at Slatey Run		700
To Doctr. William Savage pr. agreement		2500
To Robrt. Hamilton for Keeping a Blind Girl to be Left in the Churwars. hands		500
To Mary Coram a poor woman		400
To Mary Pearce a poor woman		400
To Bridget Scales a poor woman		300
To Peter Cornwell a poor man		500
To Thomas Snow a poor man		600
To Richard Johnson		500
To John Willow for keeping Nicholas Noland		400
To Benjamin Wise for his wife a poor woman		500
To Capt. William Carr pr. Acct.	₤ 11:14: 3	2900
To Thomas Chapman Ditto pr. Acct.	7:14:10	
To Thomas Lawson pr. Acct.	0: 7: 9	
To Arche. Bigbey for Repairing the Church	6: 0: 0	
To Revd. James Scott pr. Acct.	5: 0: 0	
To Jane Posey Cornish for keeping & Burieding Child	1:10: 0	
To Major Tebbs for pilchers Rent		600
To John Graham Clk.		35
To William Lane for Burring Thomas Edoo		400
To Moses Lunsford for keeping and Beruing a poor Child		600
To John Calvert pr. Acct.		500
To Moses Jeffres pr. Acct.		500

To Mr. John Simms for 2 horse Blocks	600
To William Farrow 2 Leveys overcharged	62
To William Copage for Keeping an orphan child	800
[87] To John Wellow pr. acct. 2 lbs.	
To Capt. Lewis Reno for Delikquits 1: 2: 0	
To Sarah Caster Keeping a poor Child	600
To James Eavins	600
To Mary Samson for keeping a poor Child	1000
To Elizabeth Gunn	600
To Michael Lynn for keeping Ann Shamlin	600
To William Chesher	400
To Elizabeth Lunsford for keeping a poor child	500
To Mary Wells for keeping a Blind man	1000
To Rubin Calvert	200
To John Reno for Extronary Sarvice	300
To Doct. Savage for Extrory Sarvis	600
To Thomas Moss 1 Levy over Char'd	32
To James Wilson 1 do. Do.	32
32: 8:10 at 12/6	5200
32: 8:10	47254
To 6 pr. Ct. for Collecting	2835
Cr. By 1348 tithables at 38 pr. pole 51224	50089
Remains in the Colectors hands	1135
	51224

Ordered that Colo. Henry Lee & Mr. John Hooe be Churchwardens for this present Year and that Mr. Lewis Reno be Collector on his Giving Bond and Security as Eausual.

Ordered that the above Sum of 5200 Tobo. be sold by the Collector in August Court at 12/6 per Hundred and if it ont Sell for more then cash Clamers to Receive the Tobo.

Order'd that the Church Wardens Employ workmen to make any Nessary Repairs to the Gallery at Both Churches.

Orderd. that the Churchwardens Employ workmen to Build at Each Church a House Sixteen by twelve with brick chimneys.

Order'd that the Church wardens purchas a track of Land not exceding one Hundred acres to Erect a work house on for the poor of the parish; in the meantime provide for them in the Cheapest and best maner they Can.

Signed, James Scott, Minister; Henry Lee, John Hooe, Churchwardens; Howson Hooe, Lewis Reno, William Bennett, William Carr, John Buchanon, Vest. men.

[88] At a Vestry Called and held for Dettingen Parish the 25 Day of November 1765

Present: Lewis Reno and William _____, Churchwardens; Henry Lee, Thomas Harrison, William Bennitt, John Hooe, Foushe Tebbs, William Elzey, Howson Hooe, John Buchanon, Vestrymen:

To the Revd. Mr. James Scott minister	16000
To Ditto for pr. Ct. and cask	1280
To Thomas Machen Reader at Quantico	1200
To Ditto as Clk. of the Vestry	500
To George Carter Reader at Slatey Run	1200
To John Dalton Sexton at Quantico	600
To John Willow Sexton at Slatey Run	700
To Doct. William Savage pr. agreement	2500
To William Tyler 1 Levy over Charged	32
To John Bland 1 levy over Charged	32
To Mr. John Graham pr. acct.	69
To Thomas Reves two Leveys over Charged	68
To Robert Hamelton for keeping a Blind Girl	500
To Valintine Higgs a poor man for Thomas Reves	450
To Thomas Reaves for Burying Valintine Higgs	200
To Howson Hooe pr. acct.	600
To William Coppage pr. acct.	1000
To John Riddle pr. acct. 19: 4: ½	
To Elizabeth Gunn for keeping Mathew Whaley in 1764	600
To Jane Dunlop for keeping Mathew Whaley	600
To John Calvert for keeping a Child Six month	500
To Michell Lynn for keeping Ann Shamlin	100
To Mary Corum a poor woman	400
To Moses Jeffrys for keeping & Burying John Johnson	500
To Sarah Caster for keeping Charles Shaw a Child	500
To Mary Pearce a poor woman	400
To Bridget Scales a poor woman	300
To peter Cornwell a poor man	500
To Thomas Snow a poor man	600
To William Chesser a poor man	400
To Mr. William Carr pr. acct. for parishners 8:10: 1½	
To Thomas Axell for keeping Thomas Oden a Child	750
To James Grenstead for keeping John Leader a Child	750
To Richard Johnson a poor man	500
[89] To Nicholus Nowland	400
To William Foster for keeping William Johnston child	500
To John Willow for further Service & keeping a poor woman	400
To Benjamin Wise for his wife a poor woman	500
To the Revd. Mr. James Scott pr. acct. 3: 0: 0	
To George Latham for moveing a poor woman	64
To Tobacco Levied to be Sold for cash	1500

```
                                      12: 9: 6      37725
To 6 pr. Ct. for Collecton   37725                   2263
                                                    39988
To a fraction in the Collocotors hand                 902
Cr.by 1410 thithables at 29 pr. poll               40890
                                                    40892
```

Ordered that William Carr & John Buchannon Gent. are appointed Churchwardens in this parish for the Ensuing Year.

Ordered that William Carr Gent. Collect the Levy in the Sd. parish.

Ordered that the Collector pay Humphrey Calvert the fraction in his Hands for Maintaining Sib Cornwell an orphan child.

Ordered that John Reno is appointed Clark of the Vestry.

Ordered that Lynaugh Helm Gent. be appointed Vestryman in the Rume of John Baylis being Chosen at a farmer Vestry when Six Vestrymen and the minister ware only present which Choice is hereby them moustly Confirmed by this Vestry.

Signed, James Scott, Minister; William Carr, John Buchanon, Church Wardens; Henry Lee, Thomas Harrison, Lewis Reno, Howson Hooe, John Hooe, Foushe Tebbs, William Bennitt, William Elzey.

[90] At a Vestry called and Held for Dettengin Parish the 4 day of Decembr.1767

Present: Colo. Henry Lee & John Hooe, Churchwardens; James Scott, Minister; Colo. Foushe Tebbs, Lewis Reno, Lynaugh Helm, Howson Hooe, William Carr, William Elzey, John Buchannon & Henry Peyton, Vestreymen:

DETTINGEN PARISH	Dr. lbs. Tobaco.
To the Revd. Mr. James Scott	16000
To Ditto for pr. Ct.and Cask	1280
To George Carter Reader at Slatey Run Church	2800
To Jeremiah moore Reader at Quantico	800
To John Reno Clk. of the Vestrey & processioning Sarvice	1000
To John Willow Sexton at Slatey Run	700
To Docter Savage pr. agreement	2500
To Mr. John Graham Clk.	35
To Robert Arvins Assign to Thomas Chapman	600
To George Ash one Levy over Chargd.	38
To John Halladay for Keeping Elizh. Rigg	100
To Rachal Jeffres pr. Acct.	1500
To John Dalton Sexton at Quantico part of the year 1767	300
To Benjn. Wise Sexton at Do. for the Remainder of Do.	300
To Ruth Riddle for Keeping Ann Shamlin	200
To John Willow for his wife	700
To John Willow for Keeping & Cloathing Nich. Nowland	300
To William Carr pr. Acct. 12: 3: 5 &	650
To Thos. Foulkner 2 Leveys over Chargd.	67
To the Revd. Mr. James Scott pr. Acct. 3: 4: 0	
To Jacob Calvert for Building a Vestryhouse Quantico	2800
To John Hooe for bording Elizth. Forbus 2 weaks	50
To Doct. George Graham for a visit and Medisons for Susy	100
To Elizabeth Gunn a poor woman	400
To John Catlett one Levy over Chargd.	35

```
To Edward McDonaugh for Keeping Mary Wedup 2 month          100
To Stephen pilcher a poor man                    2:10: 0
To peter Cornwill a poor man                                400
To Mary pearce a poor woman                                 400
To Thomas Snow a poor man                                   400
[91]  To Mary Sampson for Keepin. an orphan Child           400
To Benjn. Beaver for Keeping Sarah Robison                 1500
To Mary Wells for Keeping John Wells a Blind man            600
To Scarlett Maddin for Slatey Run Vestreyhouse 7/3         2750
To Tobacco Levied to be Sold to Discharge Cash             4000
To 6 pr. Ct. for Collecting 43166 Tobo.                    2589
                                    ᵼ 18:14: 5            45755
To a Frachon in the Collectors hands                       1139
                                                          46894
Cr. by Capt. Lewis Reno                        10: 7: 2     639
By 1595 Titha. @ 29 lb. Tobo. pr. poll                    46255
                                                          46894
```

Resolved that Henry Lee & John Hooe be Continued Churchwardens for the Ensuing Year.

Ordered that Each Tithable person pay John Hooe Collector 29 lb. of Tobac. pr. poll, He Given Bond and Security as Usual.

Ordered that the Churchwardens provide ornaments for the two Churches and two prayer Books.

James Scott, Minister; Henry Lee, John Hooe, Churchwarden; Foushe Tebbs, Henry Peyton, Lewis Reno, Howson Hooe, John Buchanon, Lynaugh Helm, William Carr, William Ellzey, Vestreymen.

[92] At a Vestry Called & held at Slateyrun Church the 10th of June 1768

Present: Henry Lee & John Hooe, Churchwardins; Lewis Reno, Howson Hooe, John Buchanan, Lynaugh Helm, Foushee Tebbs, Vestrymen:

Isaac Davis & Edward Williams having Returned their Report of the Lands processioned & being Examined, its ordered to be Recorded.

John Farguson & William Brown having Returned their Report of the lands processioned & being Examined, its ordered to be Recorded.

John Hancock & Thomas Rookerd having Returned their report which ordered not to be Recorded, it being an Insufficient Return.

John Peyton & John Britt having Returned their Report of the Lands processioned & being Examined, its ordered to be Recorded.

John Randolph & William Tackett having Returned a Report the said Randolph was sick & lame so that he could not comply With the Said Order in Time which was Considered as Reasonable.

Thomas Bird & William Barr having Returned their Report of the Lands processioned & being Examined, its ordered to be Recorded.

Present: William Bennett:

Isaac Farrow & Haydon Edwards having Returned their Report of the Lands processioned & being Examined, its ordered to be Recorded.

John Newman & Scarlett Maddin having Returned a Report, its thought Insufficient.

Ordered that Henry Dade Hooe be appointed Clk. to the Vestry of Dettengen Parish & that he Keep the Records accordingly.

Daniel Kincheloe & Eli Cleveland having Returned their Report of the Lands processioned & being Examined, its ordered to be Recorded.

Ordered the Churchwardins pay Capt. Scarlett Maddin fourty Nine pounds Six Shillings & Sixpence of of the Tobacco Levyed & in their hands to be sold for cash.

[93] Ordered that Lewis Reno Executor to John Reno Dec'd Deliver up all Books, Records, papers, etc. to Henry Dade Hooe Clerk of this Vestry.

Ordered that the late Churchwardens Deliver up to the Present Collector an Account of all Delinquints in this parish & him to Acct. at laying the Next levy.

Signed, Henry Lee, John Hooe, Churchwardins; John Buchanan, Howson Hooe, Lynaugh Helm, Foushee Tebbs, Lewis Reno, William Bennett.

[94] At a Vestry held for Dettengin Parish the 12th day of November 1768

Present: John Hooe and Henry Lee, Churchwardens; Lewis Reno, Foushee Tebbs, William Bennett, William Carr, John Buchanan, Lynaugh Helm, and Howson Hooe, Thomas Harrison, Vestrymen:

DETTENGEN PARISH		Dr. tobo.
To Mr. Reverend James Scott Minister		16000
To Ditto for p. Ct. and Cask		1280
To George Carter Reader at Slaty Run		1200
To Jeremiah Moore Reader at Quantico Church		1200
To Benjamin Wise Sexton at Quantico		600
To John Willow Ditto at Slaty Run		600
To Henry Dade Hooe Clerk of the Vestry		500
To Ditto for Extraordinary Service		300
To Moses Jeffress p. acct.	£ 1: 7: 6	3825
To John Riddle p.acct.	7:14: 6	
To John Hooe p.acct.		1151
To William Carr p.acct.	17: 4:11	
To Mr. Reverend James Scott p.acct.	4: 0: 0	
To John Willow p.acct.	0: 3: 0	
To Howson Hooe p.acct.	1: 0: 0	
To John Tyler p.acct.	3: 1: 0	
To Scarlitt Madden p.acct.	22:19: 6	
To Benjamin Johnson p.acct.	2: 9: 5	
To Mrs. Mary Wells a poor woman		600
To Peter Cornwill a poor man		400
To Mary Pearce a poor woman		400
To Mary Corum a poor woman		400
To Elisabeth Gun a poor woman		600
To John Willow for his wife		400
To Ditto p.acct.		120
To Stephen Pitcher a poor man		600
To Thomas Snow a poor man		600
[95] To Benjamin Beavers for Sarah Robinson		1470

To Bridget Scales Ditto		400
To Richard Johnson a poor man		400
To Joseph Carter Levies twice paid		203
To Periah Bonam Ditto		58
To Elisabeth Dean a poor woman		400
To Elisabeth Lunce for keeping a Child		600
To Doctor James Nisbett p. acct.	5: 0: 0	
To Sarah Crook for keeping Mary Crook a poor Child		400
To Mrs. Cotter for keeping a poor woman three months		150
To John Graham Clerk		64
To Mrs. Hannon		600
To Benjamin Wise for keeping fires		200
To John Willow for Ditto		200
To Henry Lee for Six Bottles of wine	£ 1:10: 0	
	£66: 0:10	35926
Tobacco to pay the Cash Claimers		8000
6 p. Ct. to the Collector		2637
		46563
27 p. Tithable		47169
Remains a fraction in the Collectors Hands of		606

Ordered that the Parish Collector pay William Oldham out of the
fraction in his hands 30 lb. Tobacco.

Ordered that Lynaugh Helm Gent. be Collector for the Ensuing
year he giving bond and Security to Henry Lee and Foushee Tebbs Gent.
and that Lynaugh Helm and Henry Lee Gentlemen be Churchwardens.

Ordered that the Said Collector Receive from each Tithable Twenty
Seven pounds of Tobacco and pay of the Different claimers and that he
sell the Eight Thousand pounds of Tobacco Leveyd. for the Cash
Claimers for the Most that can be got.

Ordered that the Collector pay out of the fraction in his hands to
Thos. Bland Ten Shillings.

Signed, Henry Lee & Lynaugh Helm, Churchwardens; Thomas Harrison,
John Hooe, Lewis Reno, Howson Hooe, Foushee Tebbs, John Buchanan,
William Bennett and William Carr.

[96] At a Vestry Called and held for Dettingen Parish the 30th day
of October 1769

Present: James Scott, Minister; Henry Lee, Henry Peyton, Thos.
Harrison, Howson Hooe, Lewis Reno, Lynaugh Helm, and Foushee Tebbs,
Vestry Men:

DETTINGEN PARISH	Dr. Tobo.
To Mr. Reverend James Scott Minister	16000
To Ditto for p. Ct. and cask	1280
To Jeremiah Moore at Quantico Church 6 months	600
To Ditto at Slaty Run	1200
To Benjamin Wise Sexton at Quantico	600
To John Willow Ditto at Slaty Run	600
To Henry Dade Hooe Clerk of the Vestry	500
To Charles Steward Reader at Quantico Church 6 months	600

	£ S d.	
To James Tebbs for finding a Coffin for Susannah Shaw	0:10: 0	
To Phillip Shaw for Diging a grave for Ditto	0: 5: 0	
To Joseph Thurman for Burying Ditto	0:10: 0	
To Joseph Thurman for keeping 4 Children one Week		50
To Phillip Shaw for keeping 3 Children and bury'g one	1: 5: 0	442
To Haden Edwards for keep'g Bridget Scales 3 Months & bury'g her	1: 5: 0	150
To John Willow for fixing a dial at Slaty Run & ferret for book	5: 6	
To Michail Lynn for keep'g & Burying Ann Shamlin	2: 0: 0	
To Abraham Raw for Burying Ann Crook	1: 5: 0	
To Benjamin Wise for Diging grave for Betty Gun	0: 2: 6	
To John Murry p. acct.	2:10: 9	
To Mrs. Jeffries p. acct.	1: 8: 0	4850
To Wm. Slade for keeping John Wells		600
To Stephen Pilcher a poor Man		600
To Thos. Snow a poor Man		600
To Doctor Graham p. acct.	8:11: 5 ¼	
To Carr & Chapman p. Acct.	11: 7: 4 3/4	
To Wm. Brown for Burying a poor Woman	1: 5: 0	
To John Willow for his Wife		400
To Benjamin Beavers for Sarah Robinson		200
[97] To Richard Johnson a poor Man		400
To Elisabeth Dean a poor Woman		400
To Elisabeth Lunce for keeping a poor Child		600
To Benjamin Wise for keeping fires at Quantico Church		200
To John Willow for Ditto at Slaty Run		200
To John Riddle p. acct. & for 4 Bottles of Wine	0:10: 0	
To the Reverend James Scott for 16 Bottles of Wine	3: 4: 0	
To Peter Cornwill a poor Man		530
To Mary Peirce a poor Woman		530
To Mary Corum a poor Woman		530
To Charles Steward for Ferrit for Books	0: 2: 0	
To Tobo. to be sold to pay the Cash Claimers		4000
To John Calvert for keeping John Tuttle a poor Child Child		
	35:19: 7	37662

Ordered that Doctor George Graham be Appointed to Administer Phisick and give his Attendance to all the Poor of this Parish whcn Called on for Which he is to Receive at the Laying of the Next Levy Lb. 2500 Tobo.

Ordered that the Churchwardens Sell the 4000 Lb. pounds of Tobo. for the best price they can git.

Ordered that Colo. Henry Peyton and Capt. Lynaugh Helm be Churchwardens Churchwardens the Ensuing Year.

Signed, James Scott, Minister; Lynaugh Helm, Henry Peyton, Lewis Reno, Howson Hooe, Henry Lee, Thos. Harrison, & Foushee Tebbs, Vestrymen.

[98] At a Vestry held for Dittingen Parish the 6th of November 1769

Present: Henry Lee, Lewis Reno, Howson Hooe, John Hooe, Linah Helm,
Wm. Ellzey & Foushee Tebbs:

DETTINGEN PARISH	Dr.
To Sundry Articles Reced. by the Vestry on Monday Last	37662
To 6 p. Ct. for the Collection	2259
	39921
To 24 p. Tithable	40968
Remains a fraction in the Collectors hands of	1047

Ordered that Colo. Peyton be Collector for the Ensuing year he
giving bond & Security to Capt. Lynaugh Helm and Majr. Lewis Reno.
Ordered that the Collector Recieve from each Tithable in this
Parish the Sum of Twenty four pounds of Tobo.
Ordered the Collector pay unto John Graham out of the fraction in
his hands 35 pounds of Tobo.
Signed, James Scott, Minister; Henry Peyton, Lynaugh Helm, Foushee
Tebbs, Howson Hooe, Lewis Reno, John Hooe & W. Ellzey, Vestm.

[99] At a Vestry Called and held for Dettingen Parish the 10th day
of Novembr. 1770
Present: James Scott, Minister; Henry Peyton & Lynaugh Helm,
Churchwardens; Henry Lee, Foushee Tebbs, Thos. Harrison, Howson Hooe,
John Hooe, John Buchanan & Wm. Ellzey, Vestrymen:

DETTENGEN PARISH	Dr. Tobo.
To the Reverend James Scott Minister	16000
To do. for p. ct. and Cask	1280
To Charles Stuart Reader at Quantico Church	1200
To Jeremiah Moore at Slaty Run do.	1200
To Benjamin Wise Sexton at Quantico for Thos. Johnson	100
To John Willow do. at Slaty Run	600
To Henry Dade Hooe Clerk of the Vestry	500
To Ann Johnson for one Months Service at Quantico	50
To John Willow Sexton at Quantico Church	450
To Mrs. Jeffres p. Acct. ₺ 1: 9: 0	2950
To William Slade for keeping John Wells	600
To Stephen Pilcher a poor Man	600
To Thomas Snow a poor Man	600
To John Willow for his Wife	400
To Judah Beverly for keep'g Sarah Robinson	600
To Richard Johnson a poor Man	400
To Elisabeth Dean a poor Woman	400
To John Willow for keeping firewood at the two Churches	400
To Peter Cornwile a poor Man	530
To Mary Pearce a poor Woman	530
To Mary Corum a poor Woman	530
To Elisabeth Lunce for keeping a poor Woman	600
To Doctor George Graham p. Agreement	2500
To Ann Stanton for keeping two poor Children	500

To Phillip Shaw for keeping Susannah Hannon   600
To Joseph Green for Removing Ann Williams   2: 8: 0
To John Leatherwood for keep'g and Cloth'g
   John Gibson & Daughters   1: 2:10   800
To James Grinstead p. Acct.   0:15: 0
[100] To Thomas Johnson for Burying Benjamin Wise   200
To John Riddle p. Acct.   11: 4: 8
To Thomas Chinn for Making two Surpluses   5: 0: 0
To Carr and Chapman p. Acct.   15: 3:10
To John Willow p. Acct.   0:12: 6
To the Reverend James Scott for 16 Bottles
   of Wine   3: 4: 0
To John Gunyan Do. for two Bottles of Wine   0: 8: 0
To James Dalton for Burying David Steward   300
To William Brent Parish Collector p. Acct.   2:12:11   192
To Hannah Russel for keeping Sarah Russel   400
To Tobo. to pay the Parish Claimers   7000
To Tobo. to be Levied and Sold for Cash towards
   Purchasing a new Gleebe   10000
To 6 p. c. for the Collector   3168

    Ordered that Colo. Foushee Tebbs and Henry Peyton be Churchwardens
the Ensuing year.
    Ordered that Colo. Tebbs be Collector the Ensuing year he giving
bond & Security to William Carr and Henry Lee.
    Ordered that W. Cuthbert Bullett be Vestrymen in the Room of
Capt. William Bennett Deceased.
    Ordered the Collector pay to John Curtess   200
    Signed, James Scott, Minister; Foushee Tebbs, Henry Peyton,
Churchwd.; Henry Lee, Thos. Harrison, Lynaugh Helm, Howson Hooe, John
Buchanan, John Hooe, William Ellzey, Lewis Reno.

    [101] At a Vestry Called and held for Dettingen Parish the 3 d. of
Decembr. 1770
    Present: Henry Peyton, Henry Lee, Lewis Reno, William Ellzey,
William Carr, Foushee Tebbs & Cuthbert Bullett, Vestrymen:

                     DETTENGEN PARISH   Dr. Tobo.

To amount Brought forward   55980
To Fraction in Collectors hands   788
                                                   56768
By 1774 Tithables @ 32 poll   56768

    Ordered that each Tithable person pay the Parish Collector Thirty
Two pounds of Tobo.
    Signed, Foushee Tebbs, Lewis Reno, William Carr, W. Ellzey, Henry
Peyton, Henry Lee & Cuthbert Bullett.

[102] At a Vestry Held for the Parish of Dettengen In the County of Prince William The Ninth day of November 1771
Present: The Reverend James Scott, Minister; Henry Lee, Lewis Reno, William Carr, William Ellzey, Cuthbert Bullett, Foushee Tebbs, Lynaugh Helm & Henry Peyton, Vestrymen & Then The Vestry Proceeded to Lay the Parish Levy.

DETTENGIN PARISH   Dr. Tobo.

To the Reverend James Scott	17280
To Charles Stewart Reader at Quantico Church	1200
To Jesse Moore Reader at Slaty Run Church	400
To Jeremiah Moore Reader at Slaty Run Church	800
To Mary Corum a poor Woman	530
To Stephen Pilcher a poor Man	600
To Peter Cornwill a poor Man	530
To Mary Pierce a poor Woman	530
To John Willow Sexton at Quantico & Slaty Run Churches	1200
To Do. for his Wife	400
To Phillip Shaw for keeping Susannah Hannon Six Months	300
To Do. for Cloathing her ᵼ 0:11: 0	
To John Willow for Mind'g the Dial at Slaty Run 0: 4: 0	
To Doctr. George Graham for the Physicking the Poor	2500
To Moses Jeffres for Accompt 6: 0: 0 &	400
To John Kelly for keeping Catharine Monroe a Bastard	550
To Doctor James Nisbitt as p. Acct.	365
To Richard Johnson a poor Man	500
To Elisabeth Lunceford for Keeping Betty Lunceford	600
To Hannah Russel for Keeping Sarah Russel	400
To William Slade for Keeping John Wells	600
To be Laid out by the Churchwardens for the use of Margret Wilkey	500
To John Randolph for Keeping Sarah Demsdell a poor Woman	100
To Leonard Milstead for Remov'g Mary Keys to the Co'ty of Fredrick a poor Woman 4: 4:10	
To John Leatherwood p. Acct. asigned to Mr. Nash 3:10: 0	
To Mary Tompson for Keeping Jean Reppito	255
[103] To Messrs. Carr Chapman & Company for Sundrys as p. Acct. Delivered In ᵼ 29:13:11½	
To Patience Bevis for Nursing Mary Bently 0:12: 0	
To William Scott for Repairs to Quantico church 0:14: 8	
To Do. for Repairing the out Steps of Quantico Church 2: 0: 0	
To Reverend James Scott for 16 Bottles of Wine 4: 0: 0	
To Mr. John Riddle p. Acct. 1: 3: 8	
To John McFee for burying a poor man 0:15: 0	

```
To John McFee a poor Man                                        300
To Michael Germin for Keep'g & burying
    Catharine Lacy                              2:10: 0
To Mr. Travers Nash for Articles furnished &
    wife & children                             7: 5: 5
To Henry Peyton for burying John Bryan          1: 5: 0
To Cumberland Wilson for Elisabeth Smith        1: 0: 0
                                              ⌐ 65: 9: 6   & 30840
```

  Ordered that William Ellzey and Howson Hooe be Churchwardens the Ensuing year.
  Ordered that Hugh Brent be Collector for the Parish of Dettengin for the Ensuing year he giving bond and Security To the Churchwardens.
  Ordered that the Vestry do Meet at the Court house of this County on the first Monday in the Next Month to finish Laying the Parish Levy.
  Signed, James Scott, Clk.; William Ellzey, Churchwdn.; Henry Lee, Henry Peyton, Foushee Tebbs, Lewis Reno, William Carr, Lynaugh Helm & Cuthbert Bullett.

  [104] At a Vestry Called and held for Dettengen Parish on the second day of December 1771
  Present: Howson Hooe and William Ellzey Churchwardens; Henry Lee, Foushee Tebbs, Cuthbert Bullitt, John Hooe, Henry Peyton & William Carr, Vestrymen:

DETTINGEN PARISH   Dr. Tobo.

```
To Sundry Articles Received by the Vestry on the
    Ninth day of November last    ⌐ 28: 0: 9       &      30840
To Henry Ravinous for burying William Strutton            300
To Henry Dade Hooe Clerk of the Vestry                    500
To George Kendall a poor Man                              600
To Joseph Thurman for keeping a poor Child 6 Months       300
To Thomas Hart for a Levey Overpaid                        30
To Thos. Snow a poor man                                  600
To Mary Collen for keeping a poor Child                   400
To John Carpenter a Levey overpaid                         30
To Tobacco to be Sold to Raise   ⌐ 28: 0: 9 @ 14/ is     4006
                                                        37606
To 6 p. c. for Collecting                                2259
                                                        39865
By 1883 Tithables at 22 lbs. Tobo. p. poll              41426
There Remains a fraction in Collectors hands of          1561
```

  On a petition of Sundry Inhabitants desiring that the Seats in the Gallery at Slaty Run church may be Sold and the Money arising from the Sale be applied towards Lessning the Next Parish Levey, it is Considered and Ordered that the Churchwardens of the Parish after giving Conveniant Public Notice Sell the Several pieus in the Said Gallery to the highest bidders and account for the Money Arising by the Sale at the Laying the Next parish Levey.

Ordered that each Tithable person pay to the parish Collector 22 pounds of Tobacco.

Signed, William Ellzey & Howson Hooe, Churchwd.; Foushee Tebbs, William Carr, Cuthbert Bullett, Henry Peyton & John Hooe, Vestrymen.

[105] At a Vestry called and held for Dittingin Parish the 7th day of November 1772

Present: Henry Lee & Howson Hooe, Churchwdns.; Foushee Tebbs, Thos. Harrison, Lynaugh Helm, Lewis Reno, John Hooe and Henry Peyton, Vestrymen:

DETTENGEN PARISH		Dr. Tobo.
To the Reverend James Scott Minister		16000
To Do. for p. C and Cask		1280
To Charles Steward Reader at Quantico Church		1200
To James Grey Reader at Slaty Run Church		1200
To Henry D. Hooe Clk. of the Vestry		500
To George Kendal a poor man assigned to Henry Peyton		600
To Thos. Snow a poor Man		600
To Mary Corum a poor Woman		530
To Stephen Pilcher a poor Man		600
To Peter Cornwil a poor Man		530
To Mary Pearce a poor Woman		530
To John Willow Sexton at the two Churches		1200
To Do. for his Wife		400
To Richard Johnson a poorman		500
To Elisabeth Lunceford for Keeping Betty Lunceford		600
To Hannah Russel for Keeping Sarah Russel		400
To Wm. Slade for keeping John Wells		600
To Tobo. To be Laid out by the Churchwdns. for ye use of Margt. Wilkey		500
To the Revd. James Scott for 16 Bottles of Wine	£ 4: 0: 0	
To John Northcutt a Levey overpaid		22
To John Dalgarn a Levey over paid		22
To John Carpenter for Levies over paid		32
To John Pierce two Levies over paid		64
To Wm. Feagins for Levies over paid		66
To Mary Ann Chesher a poor Woman		500
To Rachel Jeffres p. Acct.	1: 5: 0 &	1250
To George Bigby for Keeping Charles Stanton		600
[106] To Carr Chapman & Company p. Acct.	31:16: 5½	
To Thos. Harris p. Acct.	0:18: 6	
To Catharine Thayer Do.	0: 6: 0	
To Doctr. James Nisbitt p. Acct. for childs		1200
To John Hooe for 22 bushels of Wheat	0:12: 6	
To Henry Peyton for 12 Do. to Wilkey	0: 7: 6	
To Thos. Bland for Burying a poor Child		300
To John Calvert for Keeping a poor Child 3 months		150
To Abraham Lee a poor Man		250
To Francis Triplett for keep'g & Burying Benjamin Smith	4: 0: 0	

To Alexander Keith p. Acct.   35: 4: 8   &   866
To Elisabeth Dean a poor Woman Omitted in 1771 and the
    Present yr.   800
                                    £ 78:10: 8   33892
Tobacco Levied to Discharge 4: 0: 6 Cash Balce.   640
                                               34532

      Resolved that it be an agrement that Doctr. James Nisbett find
Medecine for the poor and that he Receive at Laying the Next Parish
Levy Twenty five Hundred Pounds of Tobo.

By Carr Chapman and Co.   £ 74: 9:12
To Six p. Ct. for Collect'g   2171
By 640 1b. Tobo. Levied for the Cash   4: 0: 6   36703
                                    78: 9: 8
To Fraction In Collectors Hands of   62
                                           36765
Cr. By 1935 Tiths. at 19 1b. Tobo. p. poll   36765

      Resolved that Howson Hooe & Henry Lee be Churchwdns. the present and
Ensuing year.
      Ordered that Hugh Brent be Parish Collector for the Ensuing year.
      Ordered that the Collector Receive from each Tithable Person 22 pounds
of Tobo. for each Levy.
      Ordered that the Churchwdns. provide for the poor of the sd. Parish.
      Signed, Howson Hooe & Henry Lee, C.W.; Thos. Harrison, Foushee Tebbs,
Henry Peyton, John Hooe, Lynaugh Helm & Lewis Reno.

      [107] At a Vestry Sumoned and held for Dettingin Parish the 27th
day of Novembr. 1773
      Present: Henry Lee & Howson Hooe, Churchwardens; Henry Peyton,
Lynaugh Helm, John Hooe, Lewis Reno, William Carr & William Ellzey,
Vestrymen:

                              DETTENGIN PARISH   Dr. Tobo.

To the Reverend James Scott Minister   16000
To Do. for p. ct. & Cask   1280
To Charles Steward Reader at Quantico Church   1200
To James Gray Reader at Slaty Run Church   1200
To Henry D. Hooe Clk. of the Vestry   500
To John Willow Sexton at the two Churches   1200
To Do. for his wife   400
To Mary Pearce a poor Woman   530
To Richard Johnson a poor man   500
To Geo. Kendal a poor Man assigned to Henry Peyton 600
To Thos. Snow a poor Man   600
To Mary Corum a poor Woman   530
To Stephen Pilcher a poor Man   600
To Peter Cornwil a poor Man   530
To Elisabeth Lunceford for Keep'g Betty Lunceford 600

```
To Hannah Russel for keep'g Sarah Russel                              400
To Mary A. Chesshire a poor Woman                                     700
To Doctor James Nisbett p. agreement                                 2500
To Rachel Jeffres p. Accompts              0;15; 0      &            1675
To Howson Hooe p. Acct.                    1: 2: 0
To Henry Lee p. Acct.                      0:12: 6
To the Reverend James Scott for 16
    Bottles Wine                           4: 0: 0
To Sylvester Moss p. Accompt                                          940
To Carr & Chapman p. Acct.                21:11: 0½      &            600
To Mrs. German for Curing Mary Turner                                 600
To John Calvert for Keep'g Jean Gibson                                600
To Abraham Lee a poor Man                                             600
To Henry Peyton for Elisabeth Dean                                    400
To Do. for Making a Coffin for Do.         0:10: 0
To Murphy Maccavoy for keep'g Mary Green & her Child                  200
[108] To James Wilkey a poor Man                                      500
To Elisabeth Gwin a poor Woman             1:19: 0
To John Willow for keep'g fires at the two Churches                   400
To Margaret Overhal for Rolley Corben      2:16: 0
To Do. for Boarding John Cane              1: 8: 0
To John Jones for Nursing Ellender Twillaven in the flux              300
To John Calvert for furnishing Jean
    Gibson                                 3: 2: 6
To William Ellzey p. Acct.                 3:12: 6
To George Bigby p. Accompt                 0:16: 0
To Doctor William Savage p. Agreement                                2500
To the Parish Collector p. Accompt         1: 8: 9      &            1197
To Thos. Montgomerie p. Acct.              0:16: 0
To William Scott p. Acct.                  0:16: 0
To Geo. Bosswel for Diging a grave for
    Mr. Pilcher                            0: 2: 6
To Do. for Supporting a base born Child 5 Months                      420
To Doctor Graham p. Accompt               20: 0: 0     _____
                                          65: 7: 9      &           40802
Tobo. to Discharge the Cash                                         20254
                                                                    61056
6 p. C. for the Collecton                                            3663
                                                                    64719
By 2017 Tiths. @ 32 lb. p. pole is                                  64544
Fraction Remaining in the Collectors hands is                         175
```

Ordered that each Tithable Person pay the Collector 32 pounds Tobacco.

Ordered that Henry Lee & Thos. Harrison be Churchwardens the ensuing Year.

Ordered that John Lee be Collector the ensuing year he giving bond & Security According to Law.

Ordered that the Churchwdns. Advertise the Glebe to be Sold in Six Months Agreable to Act of Assembly.

Ordered that the Churchwardens Imploy a Doctor on the Cheapest

Terms not exceeding 2500 pounds of Tobo. for the use of the Parish.

[109] Ordered that the 20254 pounds Tobo. Levied to pay the Cash Claimers be sold to the highest bidder & the whole amount accounted for by the Churchwardens or collector without any more than what is Allowed above for the Sale thereof.

Signed, James Scott, Minister; Lewis Reno, Howson Hooe, John Hooe, Lynaugh Helm, William Ellzey, Henry Peyton & William Carr, Vest. Men.

At a vestry Sumoned and held for Dettengen Parish ye 19th day of April 1774

Present: The Revd. James Scott, Minister; Henry Lee, Churchwarden; Henry Peyton, Lewis Reno, Howson Hooe, Lynaugh Helm, John Hooe and Cuthbt. Bullett, Vestrymen:

Ordered that Lewis Reno be Churchwarden in the Room of Colo. Thomas Harrison Deceased.

The Death of one of the Churchwardens having prevented the Sale of the Glebe according to a former Order of this Vestry, it is ordered that the present Churchwardens Sell the Same agreable to the Act of Assembly for that purpose, upon the first day of Prince William Court in Next August, and it is also Ordered that they Sell the Same upon Six months Credits taking from ye Purchasers bond with Sufficient & good Security.

Ordered that the Churchwardens advertise that any person having Lands to sell Lying about the Centre of this Parish be requested to lay a plott of the same wth. their terms before the Next Vestry to be held for this parish as the Vestry will at that time have occation to purchase a Glebe for the use of the parish.

[110] Two Vacancies being in the Vestry, one by the removal of Mr. John Buchanan, the other by death of Colo. Thos. Harrison, The Vestry proceeded to chuse in their room Mr. William Alexander & Colo. Thos. Blackburn.

Signed, James Scott, Minister; Henry Lee & Lewis Reno, Chwd.; Henry Peyton, Howson Hooe, John Hooe, Lynaugh Helm & Cuthbt. Bullett, Vestrymen.

At a vestry Summoned and held for Dettengin Parish the 5th day of December 1774

Present: the Reverend James Scott, Minister; Henry Lee, Churchwdn.; Foushee Tebbs, William Carr, John Hooe, Lynaugh Helm, Cuthbt. Bullett and Thomas Blackburn, Vestrymen:

Ordered that Cuthbt. Bullett be Appointed Churchwarden in the Room of Lewis Reno Gent. Deceased.

Ordered that the Churchwardens proceed to sell the Glebe of this parish agreable to a former order of Vestry & the Advertisements Lately Bublished for that purpose and they are hereby invested wth. the power to postpone the sale Should it appear to them it is Likely to go under the Value.

Signed, James Scott, Minister; Henry Lee, Cuthbert Bullett, Foushee Tebbs, William Carr, John Hooe, Lynaugh Helm, Thomas Blackburn, Vestrymen.

[111] At a vestry summoned & held for Dettengin Parish the 10th day

of December 1774

Present: the Reverend James Scott, Minister; Henry Lee & Cuthbert Bullett, Churchwardens; Foushee Tebbs, William Carr, Howson Hooe, John Hooe, Willm, Alexander, Thos. Blackburn & Lynaugh Helm, Vestrymen:

DETTENGIN PARISH		Dr. Tobo.
To the Revd. James Scott Minister		16000
To Do. for p. C. & Cask		1200
To Charles Steward Reader at the two Churches		2400
To John Willow Sexton at the two Churches		1200
To Henry Dade Hooe Clk. of the Vestry		500
To Mary Pearce a poor Woman		530
To Richard Johnson a poor Man		500
To George Kindal a poor man for Henry Peyton		600
To Thomas Snow a poor Man		600
To Stephen Pilcher a poor man		600
To Peter Cornwil a poor man		530
To Betty Lunceford		600
To Hannah Russel for keep'g Sarah Russel		400
To Mary anne Cheshire		700
To Abraham Lee a poor man		600
To James Wilkey a poor man		600
To Elisabeth McDonough to be Laid out by the Churchwdns.		400
To John Willow for keepg. fires at the two Churches		400
To ye Revd. J. Scott for 16 Bottles of Wine	4: 0: 0	
To William Carr p. Acct.	4: 3: 7	700
To Carr & Chapman p. Acct.	9: 6: 0	
To Edwd. Hardin a poor to be laid out by ye Churchwdns		600
To John Willow for Mending the Pews	0: 5: 0	
To Rachel Jeffres p. Acct.	0:18: 6	1200
To Elisabeth Smith a poor Woman	2: 0: 0	
To John Driskel for keeping a Child		300
To Henry Peyton for burying Kindal	1: 7: 6	
To Mrs. Chinn for Mending the Surplus	1: 5: 0	
To Wm. Carter for burying Wm. Tolford	2: 0: 0	
To Thos. Lawson for finding two three Gallon Cans	0:15: 0	
[112] To William Slade Omitted Last year	0: 5: 0	
To Simon Lutril Junr. p. Acct.	1: 0:10	
To Zelia Reno for mending a horse block	0: 5: 6	
To Docr. Nisbet p. Acct.		2500
To Do. for the Boarding Overy's Wife	2: 0: 0	
To Mr. John Lee		1846
To Sylvester Moss for Boarding a Child		800
To Henry Lee p. Acct.	2:11: 0	
To Saml. Williams for burying Mary Corum	1:10: 0	
To James King for burying Jno. Corrin	0:15: 0	
To Thos. Reno one Levy overpaid		32
	34: 7:11	36618
To 6 p. Ct. for the Collector	13:11: 6½	2197
	47:19: 5½	38815

          Ordered that each Tithable person pay the Collector Twenty pounds
of Tobacco,   40060
To fraction in the Collectors hands   1245

                                                               38815
                              CONTRA   CR

By Mr, John Lee   46:19: 5½
By Majr. Lewis Reno's Executors   1: 0: 0

                                          47:19: 5½

          Ordered that Mr. William Alexander be Churchwarden in the room Henry
Lee.
          Ordered that Mr. John Lee be Collector the Ensuing Year he giving
bond & Security as Usual.
          Ordered that Doctor J. Nisbet Administer as usual to the poor of the
Parish. Two Vacancies being in the Vestry one by death of Major Reno
& the Other by Removal of William Ellzey out of the Parish. The Vestry
Proceeded to Chuse in their Room Mr. Cuthbert Harrison & Mr. Jesse Ewell.
          Signed, James Scott, Minister; Cuthbt. Bullett & Wm. Alexander, Chwd.;
Henry Lee, Foushee Tebbs, John Hooe, Lynaugh Helm, Howson Hooe & William
Carr, Vestrymen:

          [113] At a Vestry called & held for Dittengin Parish the 21st day
of May 1775
          Present: the Reverend James Scott, Minister; William Alexander,
Churchwdn; William Carr, Foushee Tebbs, Howson Hooe, Lynaugh Helm, Henry
Peyton & John Hooe, Vestrymen:

                      DETTINGIN PARISH   Dr. Tobo.

To the Revd. James Scott Minister   16000
To Do. for p. Ct. & cask   1200
To Charles Steward Reader at the two Churches   1800
To Henry Dade Hooe Clk. of the Vestry   500
To Richard Johnson a poor man   500
To Peter Cornwil a poor man   530
To Stephen Pilcher a poor man   600
To Elisabeth Lunceford a poor Woman   600
To Hannah Russel for Sarah Russel   400
To Abraham Lee a poor Man   600
To James Wilkey a poor Man   600
To John Willow Sexton   1200
To Mary Anne Chesshire a poor Woman   700
To John Willow for keeping fires at the two Churches 400
To Elisabeth Smith a poor Woman   400
To Mrs. Margaret Rollings p. Acct.   ₺ 10:10: 0
To Docr. Forbus for Setting Willows
   leg   3:10: 0
To Henry Peyton p, Acct.   4:13:11
To Sylvester Moss for keep'g a poor Child 3 Months   150
To Do. for keeping one other poor Child 14 Months   700

                              -53-

To Do. for Burying Edwd. Lynex		150
To Mrs. Jeffres p. Acct.	5: 8: 8½	1200
To Mrs. Shoot for Delivering Ann Drue	0:10: 0	
To Jonothan Moore for Burying David Carter a poor Man		400
To Simon Luttrell Junr. p. Acct.	2:12: 6	
To John Calvert a poor Man		600
To John Curry a poor Man		600
To Robt. Forgey for Burying John Harvey		300
To Capt. Andrew Leitch p. Acct.	1:13: 2½	
[114] To Evan Williams for keeping a poor Child		800
To Bertrand Ewell for Bury. a poor person	0:17: 6	
To Capt. William Carr p. Acct.	27:17: 0	300
To Carr & Chapman p. Acct.	1:15:11	
To Lewis Reno Junr. for Boarding a poor Child		700
To Peter Cornwil a poor Man		470
To the Revd. James Scott for 16 Bottles Wine	4: 0: 0	
To John Lee Parish Collector		187
	₤ 63: 8: 9 3/4	32667

CONTRA

By John Lee Parish Collector	₤ 13:11: 6½	
	₤ 49:17: 3¼	

Ordered that William Alexander & John Hooe be Churchwardens for the present year & they with Foushee Tebbs & William Carr let out the legacy Left the Parish by Saml. Jones agreable to his Will.

Resolved that this Vestry Meet at the Next Court to Close the Levy.

Signed, James Scott; Wm. Alexander & John Hooe, Chwdn.; Foushee Tebbs, Howson Hooe, Lynaugh Helm, Henry Peyton & William Carr, Vestrymen:

[115] At a Vestry called & held for Dettengin Parish at Dumfries the first day of July 1776

Present: William Alexander & John Hooe, Churchwdns.; Henry Peyton, Howson Hooe, Lynaugh Helm, Foushee Tebbs & William Carr, Vestrymen:

DETTENGIN PARISH		Dr. Tobo.
To Amount brought forward	49:17: 3¼	32667
To John Graham Clk. for list of Tiths.		28
To Mordica Kelly for keeping a poor man	5: 5: 3	
	₤ 55: 2: 6¼	
11053 1b. Tobo. Levied to pay the above Sum @ 10/		11053
		43740

Ordered that the Churchwardens inquire into the Circumstances of James Davis & Assist him if Necessary.

To 6 p. ct. for Collecting   2626
To 1950 Tithables at 24 pounds Tobo. p. poll is   46800
                                                               46366
To Fraction in the Collectors hands   434

    Ordered that the Collector Receive from every Tithable in the Sd.
parish Twenty four pounds of Tobo. and pay the Different Claimers
herein Mentioned & that the Collector Sell the Tobo. Levied to pay
the Cash Claimer for the most it will fetch & Acct. for the same.
    Signed, James Scott, Thos. Blackburn, William Carr, Jesse Ewell,
Lynaugh Helm, Henry Peyton, Henry Lee, Howson Hooe, Cuthbt. Bullett,
Vestrymen.

    [116] At a Vestry called and held for Dittingen Parish the 13th day
of February 1777
    Present: the Reverend James Scott, Minister; Henry Lee, Howson Hooe,
Lynaugh Helm, Cuthbt. Bullett, Thos. Blackburn, Jesse Ewell, William
Carr & Henry Peyton, Vestrymen, having first taken the Oath prescribed
by Law:

	DETTENGIN PARISH	Dr. Tobo. 1b.
To the Revd. James Scott Minister		16000
To Do. for p. ct. & Cask		1280
To Charles Steward Reader at the two Churches		1800
To Henry Dade Hooe Clk. of the Vestry		500
To Richard Johnson a poor Man		500
To Peter Cornwil a poor Man		1000
To Stephen Pilcher a poor Man		600
To Elisabeth Lunceford a poor Woman		600
To Hannah Russel for Sarah Russel		400
To Abraham Lee a poor Man		600
To James Wilkey a poor Man		600
To Mary Ann Chesshire a poor Woman		700
To Alexander Humes Sexton at Slaty Run Church & for fire wood		500
To Thos. Eaves Sexton at Quantico Church & for keeping fire wood		500
To Elisabeth Smith a poor Woman		400
To Mrs. Jeffres p. Acct. 17: 4: 9 &		1200
To John Curry a poor Man to be Laid out by Capt. Carr in the Purchase of Iron & Stock		1200
To Evan Williams for keep'g a poor Child		800
To Capt. William Carr p. Acct. 8:11:11		
To Ann McAvoy for keep'g Elizth. Haywood 3: 0: 0		
To Do. for keep'g Mary Johnson 1:10: 0		
[117] To Catharine Thayor for keep'g a poor boy 4: 4: 0		
To Margaret [illegible] for keeping and Burying a poor Woman 3: 0: 0		

-55-

To Robt. Forgy for Burying Jno.
Harvy a poor Man   1: 2: 6
To the Revd. Jas. Scott for 16
Bottles of Wine   4: 0: 0 Communion
To Mary White for keep'g Jas. Brown a poor boy   500
To Zacheriah Potter a poor Man   500
                             42:13: 2
42:13: 2 Levied in Tobo. at 2 d. p. pound is   5179
                                       35359
6 p. Ct. for Collector   2122
                                       37481
1801 Tithables at 21 pounds Tobo. p. poll is   37821
To Fraction in the Collectors hands   340

      Ordered that John Hooe be Collector for Last year & this he giving Bond & Security as Usual.
      Ordered that the Collector Receive from each Tithable in this Parish Twenty one pounds Tobo. for this Present year and Pay the Different Claimers herein Mentioned & that the Collector Sell the Tobo. to pay the Cash Claimers for the most it will fetch and Acct. for the Same.
      Ordered that John Hooe and Jesse Ewell be Churchwardns. for this Present year.
      Signed, James Scott, Jesse Ewell, Thos. Blackburn, Henry Lee, Howson Hooe, Henry Peyton, William Carr & Cuthbt. Bullett, Vestrymen.

[118] At a Vestry Called and held for Dettengin the 4th day of May 1778
      Present: the Revd. Jas. Scott, Minister; Foushee Tebbs, William Carr, Henry Peyton, Thos. Blackburn, Lynaugh Helm, Cuthbt. Bullett & Henry Lee, Vestrymen:

                     DETTENGIN PARISH   Dr.

To Henry D. Hooe Clk. of the Vestry	500
To Richd. Johnson a poor man	500
To Stephen Pilcher a poor man	600
To Elizabeth Lunceford a poor Woman	600
To Hannah Russel for keeping Sarah Russel	400
To Abraham Lee a poor Man	600
To James Wilkey a poor Man	600
To Mary Ann Chesshire a poor Woman	700
To Evan Williams for keep'g a poor Child	800
To Zacheriah Potter a poor Man	500
To Elizabeth Smith a poor Woman	400
To Rebecca Barr one Levy over Charged	21
To Robt. Graham Clk. for List of Tithables	20
To Mary Wright for keep'g James Brown a poor boy	500
To James Wilkey for keep'g a poor Woman and Child Six Months	250
To Jno. Randolph for Burying a poor Man	300
To Henry Peyton for Sundry Articles Delivered to Thomas Dallis a poor Man	500

```
To William Carr p. Acct.                                            725
To Moses Moss one Levy over paid                                     21
To Doctor James Nisbett for Admisistering Medison to
    the poor of this parish at 2500 lb. Tobo. p. Annum
    for 1775 & 1776                                                5000
To Doctor Forbis p. Acct.                                          1600
To Elizabeth Whitefield for Board'g Elizabeth Haywood
    a poor Woman 9 Months                                          1025
[119] To Catharine Cox for Attend'g Judith Cooper                   150
To Christopher Bowers for Services done for H. Rawnus                55
To John Delany for Levies Overpaid for 1775 & 76                     45
```

Ordered that Colo. Jesse Ewell & Colo. William Alexander be Churchwardens for the ensuing year.

```
                                                                  ‾16412
To 6 p. ct. for collecting                                          984
                                                                  ‾17396
By 1887 Tithables at Ten pounds Tobo. p. poll                     18870
To Fraction in the collectors hands                               ‾1474
```

Ordered that each Tithable in this parish pay the Collector Ten Pounds Tobacco.

Ordered that Colo. Tebbs be Collector for the present year he giving Bond & Security as Usual.

Ordered that the Collector pay to William Scott one Hundred & fifty Pounds Tobo. out of the Fraction in his hands, William Scott having produced a proved Acct. to the Vestry for Repairs done to Quantico church for Damages it had sustained from the Enoccilation of the Continental Soldiers belonging to this State.

Ordered that the Same be Certified to the General Assembly as Reasonable.

Ordered that the Churchewardens employ for the Poor such Doctor as they may think proper.

Signed, James Scott, Minister; Henry Lee, Henry Peyton, Foushee Tebbs, Lynaugh Helm, Cuthbt. Bullett, William Carr, Thos. Blackburn, Vestrymen.

[120] At a Vesty Called & held at Dumfries the 1st day of March 1779
Present: Henry Peyton, Foushee Tebbs, Howson Hooe, Lynaugh Helm, John Hooe, Jesse Ewell & Thos. Blackburn:

DETTENGIN PARISH	Dr. Tobo. lb.
To Henry Dade Hooe Clk. of the Vestry	500
To Richd. Johnson a poor Man	530
To James Wilkey a poor Man	500
To Mary Anne Chesshire a poor Woman	700
To Eliz. Lunceford	600
To Zacheriah Potter a poor Man	500
To Eliz. Smith a poor Woman	400
To Abraham Lee a poor Man	600
To Robt. Graham Clk. for List Tithables	20
To Catherine Thayor for keeping a poor boy	216

To Evan Williams for keep'g a poor boy		800
To Rachel Jeffres p. Acct.	40;10: 0 &	600
To Hannah Russle for keep'g Sarah Russle		400
To Stephen Pilcher a poor Man		600
To John Crook a poor Man	0: 3: 1½	
To James Mooney p. Acct.	13; 9: 0	
To Absolum Crook one Levy over Charged		10
To John Hooe for furnishing J. Wood a poor		
Man wth. half a Barl. Corn	5: 0: 0	
To William Askings one Levy over Charged		10
To John Hickerson one Do. Do.		10
To Mary Wright a poor Woman		500
To Cash to be Lodged in the hands of the		
Churchwdns. to purchase Corn for the		
Poor of the Parish & if anything		
Remains in their hands to be applied		
to the parish Cred. at the Laying of		
the Next Levy.	100: 0: 0	
To Tobacco Levied to pay the cash Clamers		2500
Present: Henry Lee:		
[121] Further add for the Support of the Poor		1000
		11526
To 6 p. ct. for Collecting		691
		12217

CONTRA   Cr.

By 1788 Tiths. @ 8 lb. Tobo. p. poll	14304
Tobo. Remaining in the Collectors hands	2087

Ordered that Colo. Henry Peyton & Thomas Blackburn be Churchwardens for the present year.

Ordered that Colo. Henry Peyton Receive from each Tithable in this Parish Eight pounds Tobo.

Ordered that the Collector pay to William Scott out of the Tobo. in his hands Six pounds Currency.

Signed, Foushee Tebbs, Henry Peyton, Henry Lee, Howson Hooe, Lynaugh Helm, John Hooe & Jesse Ewell, Vestrymen.

[122] At a Vestry summoned and held for the Parish of Dettingen the 3d day of April 1780

Present: Henry Peyton, Thomas Blackburn, Henry Lee, William Alexander, Foushee Tebbs, Cutht. Bullitt, John Hooe, Jesse Ewell, Lynaugh Helm, William Carr, Gentn. of the Vestry:

DETTINGEN PARISH   Dr. lb. Tobo

To Henry Dade Hooe Clerk of the Vestry	500
To Richard Johnson a poor man	530
To James Wilkey a poor man	500
To Mary Anne Cheshire a poor woman	700
To Zachariah Potter a poor man	500

```
To Elizabeth Smith a poor woman                                    400
To Abraham Lee a poor man                                          600
To Robert Graham Clk. for List tithables                            20
To Hanah Russell for keeping Sarah Russell                         400
To Stephen Pilcher a poor man                                      600
To John Crook a poor man                                           500
To Mary Wright a poor woman                                        500
To Henry Cooper a poor man                                         500
To Thomas Parsons a poor man                                       500
To John Emmanuel a poor man                                        500
To Elizabeth Latham for keeping a poor Child                      1000
To Martha Ludwell a poor woman assigned to Moses Suthard           600
To Moses Jeffries p. Accot.                                        800
To Ditto for Wm. Millinder                                         635
To Ditto for John Robinson                                         600
[123] To Moses Jeffries for Mary Johnson                           565
To Ditto for Judy Cooper                                          1000
To Ditto for Amia Thomas                                           700
To Ditto for Elizth. Hayward                                       525
To Ditto for John Cooper                                           500
To Ditto for John Coppage                                          125
To James Achores a poor man                                        500
To James Mooney for boarding a poor woman                          200
To Thomas Chapman p. Account                                       737
To William Carr p. Account                                         122
To Mary Anne Posey a poor woman                                    500
To Mrs. Ann Downman for furnishing Mary Anne Posey with 3
    bushels Corn                                                    60
To Catherine Thayer a poor woman for the present year              500
To Dor. David Forbes p. accot.                                     800
To Wm. Scott for Mak'g a coffin for a poor child                    50
                                                                 -----
                                                                 17769
```

       The vestry is adjd. till tommorrow.

       At a vestry held for Dettingen Parish on the 2d day of May 1780
       Present: William Carr, Jesse Ewell, Thos. Blackburn, Henry Peyton,
Henry Lee, Foushee Tebbs and Cuthbert Bullitt, Gentlemen Vestrymen:
       James Nisbett Gentn. is chosen vestryman in the room of Cuthbert
Harrison Gent. deceased.
       Ordered that Mr. Evan Williams be appointed Clerk of this vestry in
the room of Mr. Henry Dade Hooe, who has removed out of this Parish and
County, and that the records & parish papers be delivered up by him to
Mr. Williams.
       Signed, Henry Peyton, Henry Lee, T. Blackburn, William Carr, Foushee
Tebbs, Cutht. Bullitt, Jessee Ewell:

       [124] At a vestry summoned and held for the parish of Dettingen the
5th Day of June 1780
       Present: James Nisbett, Henry Peyton, Thos. Blackburn, Cuthbt.
Bullitt, William Carr, Foushee Tebbs and Jessee Ewell, Gent. Vestrymen:

```
                    DETTINGEN PARISH                    Dr. lb. tobo.

To brought forward                                         17769
To Evan Williams for a cripled child                         800
To Thos. Lawson Gt. for Ł 18:15 furnished Mrs. Stubbs
    in 1778                                                  100
To Elijah Moore for keeping Anne Horton 3 months & her
    child 4 months at 50 lb. tobo. p. month each             350
                                                           19019
To 6 p. cent collecting                                     1142
To fraction                                                   13
                                                           20174
```

CONTRA   Cr.

```
By 1834 tithables at 11 lb. tobo. p. poll                  20174
```

Ordered that Henry Peyton and Thos. Blackburn gent. be continued Churchwardens for the ensuing year.

Ordered that the Sheriff collect of each tithable person in this parish Eleven pounds of tobacco and pay the several Claimants.

Signed, Henry Peyton, T. Blackburn, Jas. Nisbett, Jesse Ewell, Foushee Tebbs, Cutht. Bullitt, William Carr.

[125] At a Vestry summoned & held for Dettingen Parish in the County of Prince William the 3d day of April 1781

Present: Henry Peyton, Thomas Blackburn, Henry Lee, Foushee Tebbs, Cutht. Bullitt, William Carr & Jesse Ewell, Gentlemen Vestrymen:

```
                                                          lb. Tobo.

To Evan Williams Clerk                                       500
To Richard Johnson a poor man                                530
To Marianne Cheshire a poor woman                            700
To Zachariah Potter                                          500
To Elizth. Smith to be paid Capt. Carr for her support       400
To Abraham Lee to be paid Wm. Nally                          600
To Robt. Graham Clk.                                          20
To Hannah Russell for keeping Sarah Russell                  400
To Stephen Pilcher                                           600
To John Crook a poor man                                     800
To Mary Wright a poor woman                                  500
To Henry Cooper a poor man                                   500
To Thos. Parsons Ditto                                       500
To Elizth. Latham for keeping a poor child                   600
To Cat. Thayer a poor woman                                  500
To Evan Williams for a cripled child                         800
To Moses Jeffries p. account                                5568
To John Bayes a poor man                                     275
To John Mucklebury                                           400
                                                           14693
```

-60-

To Fras. Cornwell board'g Ben. Adams 1 Month		200
To Wm. Carr gt. for 33 yds. Ozns.		825
		15718
To 6 p. Ct. Collecting		950
		16668
To fraction		495
		17163

Cr.

By 1907 tithes at 9 lb. Tobo. p. poll   17163

[126] Ordered that the sherif collect for each tithable person in the parish 9 lb. Tobo. p. poll and pay the several Claimants.

Jesse Ewell and James Nisbett gentn. are appointed Churchwardens for the ensuing year.

H. Lee, Henry Peyton, Foushee Tebbs, T. Blackburn, William Carr, Cutht. Bullitt, Jessee Ewell.

At a Vestry summoned and held for the Parish of Dettingen in the County of Prince William the 2nd day of April 1782

Present: James Nisbett, Henry Lee, Fousheee Tebbs, Thomas Blackburn, John Hooe, Cutht. Bullitt, Jesse Ewell, William Carr, Gentlemen Vestrymen:

DETTINGEN PARISH		Dr. tobo.
To Evan Williams Clerk of the Vestry		500
To Richard Johnson a poor man		530
To Maryanne Cheshire a poor woman		700
To Zachariah Potter		500
To Elizth. Smith to be paid Capt. Carr for her support		400
To Abraham Lee to be paid Wm. Nally		600
To Robt. Graham Clerk		20
To Stephen Pilcher		600
To John Crook a poor man		600
To Mary Wright for a poor woman		500
To Thomas Parsons		500
To Elizth. Linch for keeping a poor child		600
To Catherine Thayer		500
To Evan Williams for a cripled Child		800
To Moses Jeffries p. account	⊥ 1: 4: 9	2900
[127] To John Bayes a poor man		275
To John Mucklebury		400
To John Delany p. accot. proved	1: 5: 6	
To Geo. Earle for his afflicted wife		500
To John Mooney for keeping a child two years		1000
To Elijah Calvert p. accot.		250
To Sarah Dial Do.		600
To Dor. David Forbes p. accot.		800
To Dor. Jas. Nisbett for all former accounts		3360
		17435

```
To be sold by the Collr. to discharge the Cash debts          500
To 6 p. Ct, for Collecting                                   1080
To Hannah Russell for Sarah Russell                           400
                                                            ------
                                                            19415
To fraction in Collr's. hands                                1617
                                                            ------
                                              1b.           21032

                                                              Cr.

By 1912 Tithables at 11 1b. tobo. p. Tith.    1b.          21032
```

Ordered that the Sheriff be Collector for the present year after giving Security for faithful performance.

Ordered that James Nisbett and Jesse Ewell Gent. be Churchwardens for the ensuing year.

Foushee Tebbs, James Nisbett, Cutht. Bullitt, Jesse Ewell, Will. Carr, John Hooe, T. Blackburn.

[128]   At a Vestry held for the parish of Dettingen in the County of Prince William at the house of Mr. John Randolph's in the said County the 1st day of Octor. 1782

Present: Henry Lee Esqr., Howson Hooe, John Hooe, Lynaugh Helm, Jesse Ewell, William Alexander, Cutht. Bullitt and Thos. Blackburn, Gent. of the Vestry:

The above Gentlemen took the several Oaths prescribed by Law which oaths were administered by James Ewell Gt. one of the Justices of the peace for the said County.

The Vestry then proceeded to the Election of a Minister for this parish in the room of the late reverend Jas. Scott decd. and unanamiously made choice of the Revd. John Scott as Minister of the same.

Thomas Fitzhugh gt. is unanimously appointed a Vestrymean of the parish of Dettingen in the room of Henry Peyton gt. deced. & took the oaths accordingly.

Signed, H. Lee, Howson Hooe, John Hooe, Lynaugh Helm, Cutht. Bullitt, Wm. Alexander, T. Blackburn, Jesse Ewell.

[129]   At a Vestry held for the Parish of Dettingen in the County of Prince William at the House of John Cheek the 3d day of May 1783

Thomas Fitzhugh Gent. Came into Vestry and Subscribed that he would be comfortable to the rights and Ceremonies of the Church of England as practiced within this Commonwealth.

Present: John Scott, Minister; Henry Lee, Foushee Tebbs, William Carr, Cuthbert Bullitt, William Alexander, Jesse Ewell, Thos. Fitzhugh Gent.

Willoughby Tebbs Gent. is appointed Clerk of this Vestry.

DETTINGEN PARISH   Dr. 1b. Tobacco

```
To Mr. Evan Williams Late Clerk of the Vestry Deceased        500
To Richard Johnston a Parishioner to be pd. into the
     hands of Capt. Carr                                      530
```

To Mariana Cheshire a Poor Woman	700
To Zachariah Potter	500
To Elizabeth Smith Paid to Wm. Carr for her Support	400
To Abraham Lee a Poor Man	400
To Robert Graham Clerk	20
To Stephen Piltcher	600
To John Crook	600
To George Barker for Abraham Lee	200
To Thomas Parsons	500
To Elizabeth Finch for keeping John Hazelrig a Poor Child	600
To Catharine Thayer a Poor Woman	500
To Evan Williams for keeping Richd. Williams a Cripled Child	800
[130] To Moses Jefferies per Acct.	1278
To Mary Robertson for keeping John Muckelbury	400
To Do. for burying him	200
To George Earls for his Wife	300
To George Barker per Acct.	300
To Catherine Davis for keeping Saml. Horton a Poor Child	200
To Philip Shaw for Do.	300
To Elizabeth Lunchford for keeping a Cripled Child	400
To John Randolph for burying Margarit Wilkey	200
To Colo. Jesse Ewell for Necessaries found Do.	200
To Elizabeth Snow a Poor Woman	600
To Baptist Cheshire for keeping Mary Williamson & child Pr. Acct.	475
To Charles Shury for burying Elisabeth McCray & Nursing Do.	350
To William Slade Pr. Acct.	200
To Anne Pines Brent Do.	320
To John Delany for keeping Wm. Milliner & find'g a pr. of Shoes	650
To Carr & Chapman Pr. Acct.	569
To William Carr Pr. Do.	100
To Mr. Alexander Lithgow Do.	516
To Eleanor Thomas Do.	25
To Hannah Russel for keeping Sarah Russel for the year 1782	400
	14833

Ordered that the Church Wardens of Dettingen Parish Send to the Poor House, keep by Moses Jefferies, Abrahm Lee, Catherine Thyer & Isabel Mitchell & any other that may in future Apply that they may think Objects of Charity.

Foushee Tebbs & Thos. Fitzhugh Gent. are appointed Church Wardens.

John McMillion Gent, is appointed Vestrayman for the Parish of Dettingen in the Room of James Nisbitt Gent. Deceased & took the Oaths prescribed by Law & thereupon came into Vestry & Subscribed [131] to be Comfortable to the Rights & Ceremonies of the Church of England as Practiced within this Commonwealth.

John McMillion, Henry Lee, Foushee Tebbs, William Carr, Cuthbert Bullitt, William Alexander, Jesse Ewell, Thomas Fitzhugh.

At a Vestry held for the Parish of Dettingen the County of Prince William at the house of William McDaniels in the Said County the 5th day of May 1783
Present: Henry Lee, Foushee Tebbs, William Carr, Cuthbert Bullitt, Jesse Ewell, Thomas Blackburn & John McMillion Gent.:
Ordered that Foushee Tebbs Gent. be Appointed Collector given bond & Security.

DETTINGEN PARISH	Dr. Tobacco
Dr. Brought Over	14833
To 6 pr. C. Commission Collecting	890
To the fraction that will be in the Hands of Col. Foushee Tebbs	1166
	16889

Contra	Cr.
By Fraction in the Hands of Wickliff & Neal, D.S.	1905
By 1873 Tithes @ 8 lb. Pr. Poll	14984
	16889

Ordered that the Collector Receive from each tithable Person the Sum of Eight Pounds of Tobacco Pr. Poll.
Foushee Tebbs, Cuth. Bullitt, Thomas Blackburn, Jesse Ewell, William Carr, Henry Lee, John McMillion.

[132] At a Vestry held for the Parish of Dettingen in the County of Prince Willm. at the Clerks Office of the Said County, the 6th Day of April 1784
Present: Henry Lee, Foushee Tebbs, Howson Hooe, Cuthbert Bullitt, Jesse Ewell, William Carr & Thomas Fitzhugh:

DETTINGEN PARISH	Dr. lb. Tobo.
To Willoughby Tebbs Clerk	500
To Richard Johnston a Poor Man	530
To Mariana Chesshire a Poor Woman	700
To Zachariah Potter a Poor Man	500
To Elizabeth Smith (to be pd. Capt. Carr for her Support)	500
To Robt. Graham Clerk for the List of Tithes	20
To Stephen Pilcher a Poor Man	600
To John Crook Ditto	600
To Thomas Parsons Ditto	500
To Catharine Thyer (to be pd. Capt. Carr)	500
To Sarah Williams for keeping Richd. Williams a Cripple	800
To Moses. Jeffries p. Acct.	1200
To George Earls for his Wife (200 lb. of it for J. Fonworthy)	500

To Elizabeth Lunchford for keeping a Cripled Child   400
To Elizabeth Snow a Poor Woman   600
To John Dulany for keeping Wm. Miliner a Poor Man   600
To William Carr Gent. p. Acct.   833
To Hannah Russell for keeping Sarah Russell   400
To George Latham a Poor Man   530
To John Dulany for keeping Mary Miliner   50
To Catharine Hees for nursing her Mother   100
To John Thurman for keeping John Bayse & Wife   800
To Philip Shaw for keeping Saml. Horton & Orphan   450
To Robert Hamlinton for keeping Ann Hamlinton   400
To Michael Coon for keeping Rebecca Williamson a Child   300
To Colo. Henry Lee p. Acct.   125
To Philip Dawe p. Acct.   935
To Thomas Chapman p. Acct.   88
To Purchase Grain to Relieve the Immediate Necessities
   of the Poor to be Lodged in the Hands of the
   Churchwardens for that Purpose who are to take
   Bonds from those furnished for the Repayment of the
   Same   10000

[133] DETTINGEN PARISH   Dr. lb. Tobo.

To Debit Brought up	23961
To 6 p. C. for Collecting 23961 lb. of Tobo.	1438
To Fraction in he Hands of the Collector	1446
	26845

Contra   Cr.

By 2065 Tithes at 13 lb. of Tobo. p. Poll   26845

    Ordered that the Collector Receive from each Tithable Person thirteen pounds of Tobacco & pay the Several Claimants.
    Ordered that Foushee Tebbs & Thomas Fitzhugh Gents. be Continued Church Wardens for this Present year.
    Ordered that the Church Wardens be appointed Collectors unless the Sheriff is by Law Collector and in the last Case that he give Bond to the Church Wardens for the Due Performance of the Same.
    Signed, H. Lee, Foushee Tebbs, Will. Carr, Cutht. Bullitt, Jesse Ewell, Howson Hooe, Thomas Fitzhugh, Gentn. of the Vestry.

    At a Vestry held for the Parish of Detingen in the County of Prince William at the House of Mr. John Cheek on Saturday the 22nd Day of May 1784
    Present: Henry Lee, Thos. Blackburn, Howson Hooe, Jesse Ewell, Foushee Tebbs, John Hooe, Lynaugh Helm, John McMillian:
    Then the Vestry Proceeded to the Election of a Minister in the Room of the Revd. John Scott who has Resigned & thereupon Unanimously Made Choice of the Revd. Spence Grayson as Incumbent & Minister of this Parish.

John Thornton Fitzhugh Esqr. is appointed a Vestrayman of this Parish in the Room of Thomas Fitzhugh Esqr. Who has Removed who thereupon took the oath & in Presence of the Vestry Subscribed to be Conformable to the Liturgy of the Church of England as Established by Law.

John Thornton Fitzhugh Esqr. is appointed Church Warden for this Present Year in the Room of Thomas Fitzhugh Esqr.

Signed, Henry Lee, Foushee Tebbs, Howson Hooe, John Hooe, Lynaugh Helm, Thomas Blackburn, Jesse Ewell & John McMillian.

[134] At a Vestry held for the Parish of Dettingen in the County of Prince William at the House of Mr. John Cheek on thursday the 27th of January 1785

Present: Henry Lee, William Carr, Howson Hooe, Jesse Ewell, John Hooe, Will. Alexander & John Fitzhugh, Gentlemen Vestrymen:

DETTINGEN PARISH	Dr. lb. of Tobo.
To Willoughby Tebbs Clerk of the Vestry	500
To Richard Johnston a Poor Man	530
To Marian Cheshire a Poor Woman	700
To Zachariah Potter a Poor Man	500
To Eliz. Snow a Poor Woman	400
To Robt. Graham Cl. Acct. for the List of Tithes	20
To John Crook a Poor Man	600
To Thomas Parsons Do.	500
To Catharine Thyer (to be pd. Capt. Carr)	500
To Sarah Williams for keeping Richd. Williams a Cripple	800
To Moses Jeffries for Do. Mary Johnston & Wm. Miliner	1200
To Do. p. Account	60
To George Earls	500
To Eliz. Lunch	400
To Eliz. Snow	600
To Robert Hamlinton (for keeping Ann Hamlinton)	400
To Samuel Williams for Nursing and Burying Elor Ealse	300
To Doctor David Forbes p. Acct.	825
To James Williams for keeping 2 Small Children	1200
To Charles Shury for keeping Mary Neale	130
To William Carr Gent. p. Account	1049½
To William Tackett p. Do.	75
To Elias Ashby a Poor Man	500
To Mary Russell for Keeping her Daughter	600
To James Wilkey a Poor Man	400
	13309½
To 6 p. C. for Collecting 13309½ lb. of Tobo.	796
To Fraction in the Hands of the Collector	335½
	14441

CONTRA	Cr.
By 2063 tithes @ 7 lb. of Tobo. p. Poll	14441

[135]   Ordered that the Collector Receive from each Tithable
Person the Sum of Seven Pounds of Tobacco & pay the Several Claimants.
    Ordered that the Sheriff be Appointed Collector.
    Ordered that William Carr and John Fitzhugh Esqr. be appointed
Church Wardens for the Present Year.
    Ordered that Isaac Wickliffe pay into the Hands of the Church
Wardens the 10,000 pounds of Tobacco Levied Last Year & that
Willoughby Tebbs Render into the Hands of the Church Wardens all Bonds
& Notes taking by Foushee Tebbs Gent. Late Church Warden for this Parish.
    Ordered that the Members of the Episcopal Church meet on Monday
in Easter Week for the Purpose of Electing a Vestry Agreable to an
Act of Assembly in That Case Made & Provided.
    Signed, John Fitzhugh, William Carr, Henry Lee, Howson Hooe, John
Hooe, Wm. Alexander, Jesse Ewell.

    [136 blank, 137]   The following Gentlemen being Returned as duly
Elected for the Parish of Dettingen under an Act of Assembly intitled
an Act for incorporating the protestant episcopal Church Viz: Henry
Lee, Howson Hooe, John Hooe, William Carr, William Alexander, John
Kincheloe, Richard Neale, Henry Washington, James Gwatkin, Isaac
Wickliffe, Bernard Hooe & John McMillion, Vestrymen.
    We the Subscribers being elected as Vestrymen of the protestant
episcopal Church do Declare that we will be Comformable to the
doctrines, Discipline and Worship of the said protestant Church.
    Present: Henry Lee, Howson Hooe, John Hooe, William Alexander,
John Kincheloe, Richard Neale, Henry Washington, James Gwatkin,
Isaac Wickliffe, Bernard Hooe & John McMillion.

    [138]   At a Vestry called & held for Dettingen Parish the 2d day
of May 1785
    Present: Henry Lee, Howson Hooe, John Hooe, William Alexander,
John Kincheloe, Richard Neale, Henry Washington, James Gwatkin,
Isaac Wickliffe, Bernard Hooe, John McMillion, Vestrymen.
    The Vestry proceeded to the Choice of laiman agreeable to the
Sd. Act to Represent them in General Convention and do Unanimously
Nominate and Appoint Colo. Jesse Ewell who is Requested to Accept of
the Same.
    Ordered that the Late Clerk deliver to the Present Clerk all the
Books & Records belonging to this Parish to the Present Clk.
    Henry Lee and Howson Hooe are Appointed Churchwardens for ye
present year.
    Mr. John Hooe Junr. is appointed Clerk of this Vestry.
    Signed, Henry Lee, Howson Hooe, Churchwardens; John Hooe, William
Alexander, John Kicheloe, Richard Neale, Henry Washington, James
Gwatkin, Isaac Wickliffe, Bernard Hooe and John McMillion Gentn. of
the Vestry.

    [139]   At a Vestry called and held for the Parish of Dettingen in
the house of Mr. Wm. Tebbs in Dumfries 5th of September 1785
    Present: the Reverend Spence Grayson, Minister; Henry Lee &

Howson Hooe Churchwardens; John Hooe, Wm. Alexander, John Kincheloe, Richd. Neale, Henry Washington, Isaac Wickliffe & Jas. Gwatkin, Vestrymen:

The Vestry do Recommend to each of the Members of Vestry to advance to Colo. Jesse Ewell Eight Shillings & four pence apiece to be paid by him the the Legates sent from the Convention of the protestant episcopal Church to the General Convention which are shortly to meet in Philadelphia.

It is Recommended also that the further sum of Eight Shillings & four pence be paid by the Vestry to Colo. Jesse Ewell for his Expences in Convention.

The Vestry do Unanamously appoint Colo. Jesse Ewell there Delegate to Represent them the Next General Convention of the Protestant Episcopal Church.

Ordered that the Several members of the Vestry hand about Subscriptions & Make Collections for the Support of the Protestant Episcopal Church, also Subscriptions to be Offer'd for the Support of the Minister.

Ordered that Colo. Henry Lee & William Alexander wait on Mr. Cuthbert Bullitt & take such Security for Six Hundred pounds Left by Saml. Jones Deceas'd to the Vestry of Dettingen Parish as the Said Jones's Will Directs & Settle the Interest thereof.

Signed, Spence Grayson, Minister; Henry Lee & Howson Hooe, Churchwardens; John Hooe, Wm. Alexander, John Kincheloe, Richd. Neale, Henry Washington, Isaac Wickliffe and James Gwatkin, Gentn. of the Vestry.

MINUTES OF MEETINGS OF THE
OVERSEERS OF THE POOR, 1788-1802

OVERSEERS OF THE POOR

[140 blank, 141]   At a Meeting of a Majority of the Overseers
of the Poor at the Court House in Dumfries agreable to Law this first
day of September 1788
     Present: Howson Hooe Esqr., John Hooe Esqr., John Fitzhugh Esqr.,
William Carr Esqr.:
     Ordered that Howson Hooe Esqr. be appointed President.
     Ordered that Henry D. Hooe be appointed Clerk.
     Ordered that the poor of the said County be informed that a Meeting
will be at Lewis Reno's in the said County on the last Thursday in
October when the Overseers of the Poor will proceed to Business.
     Signed, Howson Hooe, John Hooe, John T. Fitzhugh, William Carr.

     At a Meeting of the Overseers of the Poor called and held in the
House of Lewis Reno in the County of Prince William and Parish of
Dettingin the 30th of October 1788
     Present: Howson Hooe, President; John Hooe & William Carr:

To Elisabeth Shurley a poor Woman	600
To Johnson Owings a Cripple	1200
To Richd. Shurly for keep'g Wm. Shurley a blind Man	1200
To Robt. Hamilton for keep'g Anne Hamilton a blind Girl	1000
To John Baize and Wife two poor people	1000
To Thos. Bristoe for keep'g John Willow a blind Man	1000
[142] To Elizabeth Doubty for keep'g Eliza. Wood an Idiot	600
To Clement Fare a poor Man	400
To John Casey a poor Man	500
To Sarah Durmon a poor Woman	600
To Levina Croson a poor Woman	600
To Elizabeth Steward for keeping her Sickly Son	600
To Isaac Hamrick for keeping Jno. Hamrick an Idiot	600
To Danl. Paris for keeping Anne Paris to be pd. to Isabel Forbus	600
To Jacob Lannon for keeping a Child wth. Fitts	600
To Anne Earls a poor Woman	600
To William Drury a poor Man	600
To John Simpson a poor Man to be pd. to C. Campbell	600
To Ignatious Peake a poor Man	600
To Mary Turner a poor Woman	500
To William Martin a poor Man	400
To John Smith for keeping Mary Cristia	300
To Anne Williams a poor Woman	600
To Margaret Barker for keeping Betty Bunn	600
To Elizabeth Nelson for keeping her Crippled Child	500
To Mary Anne Posey a poor Woman	500
To John Cornhil and Wife two poor people	500

```
To Saml. Pickril for keeping a Child with Fitts              600
To Robt. Bird a poor Man                                     600
To John Foxworthy for keeping his Son                        600
To Sarah Williams for keeping a Crippled Boy                 600
To Barbara Forscythe a poor Woman Dead bury'g                300
To William Wright for keep'g Js. Wilkey 4 Months             200
To Mary Mickleberry a poor Woman                             600
To Moses Jeffres p. Acct.                     8: 2: 6       1200
To Henry Dade Hooe Clk.                       5: 0: 0
To George Lampkin for keep'g Ann Horton & Child 1 Month      200
To James Webster for keep'g three poor Children             1800
To Moredock McKinny a poor Man & his Wife                    300
To William Scott for keeping Mary Moore 3 Months             150
To Robt. Hedges for keeping Eliza. Moore's Child             600
[143] To Mrs. Ashby for Supporting a Crippled Child          600
To Doctor Forbus p. Acct.                                   2509
To Doctor Campbell p. Do.
To William Carr p. Acct. Sundries furnished the Poor
   of the lower District                     12: 3: 2
                                             25: 5: 8      27659
£ 25: 5: 8 in Tobacco at 16/8 p. ct. is                     3034
To William Wyatt p. Acct. 1:17: 9 in Tobo. at 2d is          227
                                                           30920
To the Sheriff for Collection                               1856
                                                           32776
3330 Tithables at 10 p. poll is                            33330
Fraction in the Collectors hands                             554
                                                           32776
```

At a Meeting of the Overseers of the Poor of the County of Prince William Continued from the 30th of October 1788

Ordered that the Sheriff of Prince William County Collect from the Several Tithable persons or owners of such Tithables Ten pounds of Tobacco or one Shilling and eight pence Optional to the payor and pay the same to the Different Claiments According to Law this 1 Dec. 1788

Signed, John McMillion, William Carr, John T. Fitzhugh & James Ewell.

Note discovered there is an error in the addition of the above Tobo.

[144] At a Meeting of the Overseers of the poor at Dumfries agreable to Law the 7th September 1789

Present: Colo. William Alexander, Colo. Jesse Ewell, Mr. James Gwatkin, Mr. John Kincheloe, Mr. Bernard Hooe & Mr. James Grinstead, Overseers of the poor:

Ordered that Colo. William Alexander be appointed president.

Ordered that Mr. Henry Dade Hooe be appointed Clerk.

Ordered that the Clerk advertise a Meeting of the Overseers of the poor to be held at the House of Mr. Lewis Renoe on Friday the 25th of September Next to inquire into the Situation of the poor within the

County of Prince William.
     Signed, William Alexander, Jesse Ewell, Bernard Hooe, James
Gwatkin, James Grinstead & John Kincheloe.

     [145] At a Meeting of the Overseers of the poor for the County
of Prince William under the Act of Assembly inititled an Act to
provide for the poor of the Several Countyies within the commonwealth
at the House of Mr. Lewis Renoe on Friday the 25th of September 1789:
     It is considered that the Several Sums of Tobacco hereafter
Mentioned be Levied for the following persons to Wit:

To Johson Owens a Cripple	1000
To Richard Shurley for keeping Wm. Shurley a blind Man	1000
To Robert Hamilton & Daughter two poor people	1000
To John Baize & Wife two poor people	1000
To Thos. Bristow for keep'g Jno. Willow a blind Man	1000
To Doubty for keep'g Eliz. Wood an Idiot	600
To Climant Faire a poor Old Man	400
To John Casey a poor Old Man	800
To Levina Croson a poor Old Woman	600
To Elisabeth Steward for keep'g a Sickly Boy	600
To Isaac Hamrick for his son an Idiot	600
To Isbel Forbis for keeping Paris's Daughter	800
To Jacob Lannum for his Fittified Daughter	800
To Anne Earls a poor Woman	500
To Sarah Williams for keep'g Rd. Williams	400
To Mary Muckleberry	400
To Moses Jeffris p. Acct.	1350
To James Webster for keep'g 3 poor Children	1800
To Moredock McKinsy & Wife 2 poor people	300
To Robert Hedges for keeping a helpless Child	600
To Johns Simpson a poor Man	400
To James Grinstead for Burying Ignatius Peake	300
To Mary Turner a poor Woman	500
To Anne Williams a poor Woman	600
To Margret Barker for keep'g Mary Byrn	600
To Elisabeth Nelson for keeping her Child	500
To Mary Posey a poor Woman	500
To John Cornhill & Wife two poor People to be laid out by John Grinstead	800
To Robert Bird blind Man	600
[146] To John Foxworthy for his son	600
To James Ganett for Burying a poor Man	300
To Gerrard Anderson for keep'g Mary Neale	400
To Moses Garrison for keep'g Mary George	600
To James Bryan for keeping a Mad woman	150
To William Ennis for keeping a poor Child	600
To Ignatious Godwood for keeping an Idiot	800
To Anne Stanton a Sickley & poor Woman	600
To Peter Smith for keeping Elizabeth Waller and three Children 3 Months	500

To Elizabeth Hurley a poor aged Woman   500
To George Appleby for keeping 2 Children   1000
To Andrew Brown a poor Man   400
To William Martin for keep'g J. McIntosh   400
To Nancy Sinclair for keep'g a blind Woman   800
To Jane Cheshire for keeping a Base born Child   600
To James Fullum a poor Man   400
To Moses Jeffres p. Acct.   49: 4: 0
To William Carr p. Acct.   19:12:10
                                                   ────────   ─────
                                                   68:16:10   29000

The president & Overseers have postponed the Closing the Levy till
the 3d Day of November Next when they are to be Convened at the House
of John Shute in the Town of Dumfries for that purpose.
    Signed, William Alexander, Bernard Hooe, Jesse Ewell, James Gwatkin,
James Grinstead & John Kincheloe, Overseers of the Poor.

    [147] At a Meeting of the Overseers of the Poor at the House of
John Shute in the Town of Dumfries on the 3d day of Novr. 1789
    Present: Colo. William Alexander, President; Mr. Bernard Hooe,
Mr. James Gwatkin, Mr. James Grinstead, Mr. John Kincheloe & Colo.
Jesse Ewell, Overseers of the Poor:

To Tobacco Allowed sundrey poor Persons together with
    Sundry Accts. Recd. on the 25th of Sepr. last   29000
To Anne Earls for keep'g Jane Chesshire 1 Month   100
To James Grinstead for keep'g a blind Woman   1000
To Colo. Jesse Ewell for Burying Edwd. Oneale   300
To Jeremiah Dowell for Burying a poor Man   300
To the Amt. of Cash Recd. on the 25th
    Sepr. last   68:16:10
To Doctr. William Graham p. Acct. Doct.
    to   10: 0: 0
To Dr. George Graham p. Acct.
    Doct. to   2: 8: 0
To Do. Do.   1:10: 0
To Henry Dade Hooe Clerk   5: 0: 0
                                                   ────────   ─────
                                                   87:14:10   30700
To Tobacco to pay of the Cash Claimers   10529
                                                                             ─────
                                                                            41229
To 6 p. Ct. on 41229 is   2473
                                                                             ─────
                                                                            43702
Credt. By 3320 Tithables at 14 lb. Tobo. pr. poll   46480
the Remain'g Fraction in Collectors hands is   2778
                                                                             ─────

    Ordered that the Sheriff Receive from ea. Tith, in ye Coty. 14
lb. of Tobacco or 2/4 at the Option of the payor.
    Ordered that Colo. William Alexander, Colo. Jesse Ewell & Mr.
Bernard Hooe or any two of them wait on Mr. Cuthbert Bullitt and take
such security on Samuel Jones's Donation as the said Jones's Will
Directs, Settle the interest due and Receive the same.

Ordered that the above Gentlemen wait also on Mr. Carr to Settle his Acct. and Receive the Balance due.

Signed, William Alexander, Bernard Hooe, James Gwatkin, Jesse Ewell, Js. Grinstead & Jno. Kincheloe.

[148]   At a meeting of the Overseers of the Poor agreable to Law on the Sixth day of September in the Town of Dumfries

Present: Colo. William Alexander, President; Colo. Jesse Ewell, Capt. Bernard Hooe & Mr. James Grinstead & finding it not convenient to proceed to business have adjourned to Friday the 15th of October 1790 at the House of Mr. Cheek. The Clerk is directed to give Public Notice that the Overseers are to be convened at the above time to inquire into the Situation of such Poor persons as may then apply for Relief and for other Business.

Signed, Wm. Alexander, Jesse Ewell, Bernard Hooe, James Grinstead.

October 15 1790 their not being a Sufficient Number of Members present to Constitute a meeting the business is postponed to the 13th Novr. 1790 when the meet'g is to be held at Lewis Reno's on the 13 November 1790.

At a Meeting of the Overseers of the Poor at the House of Lewis Reno on the 13th of November 1790 agreable to adjournment

Present: Colo. William Alexander, president; Colo. Jesse Ewell, James Grinstead, John Kincheloe and Capt. James Gwatkins, Overseers of the Poor

To Johnson Owings a Cripple	1000
To Richrd. Shurley for keeping Wm. Shurley a blind Man	1000
To Robert Hamilton and Daughter two poor persons	1000
To John Baize and Wife two poor persons	1000
To Thomas Bristow for keeping John Willow	1000
To Elizabeth Doubty for keeping Eliz. Wood an Idiot	600
To Climent Fare a poor Man	400
To John Casey a poor Man	800
To Levina Crowson a poor Woman	600
To Isaac Hamrick for keeping his Silly Son	600
To Isbel Forbis for keeping Daniel Paris's Daughter a poor Girl	1000
[149] To Jacob Lannum for keeping his Fittified Daughter	600
To Anne Earls a poor Woman	500
To Sarah Williams for keeping Richd. Williams	400
To Mary Muckleberry a poor Woman	400
To Robert Hedges for keeping a helpless Child	800
To John Simpson & Wife two poor People	700
To Mary Turner a poor Woman	500
To Anne Williams a poor Woman	600
To Margret Barker for keeping Nancey Byrn	600
To Mary Posey a poor Woman	500
To John Cornhil & Wife two poor People to be paid to James Grinstead	1000

```
To John Foxworthy for his Son                                600
To William Ames for keeping a poor Child                     600
To Ignatious Godwood for keeping an Idiot                    800
To Elisabeth Hurley a poor Woman Dead                        500
To Sarah Calvert for keeping James McIntosh                  400
To Elizabeth Stephens for keeping a poor Woman               800
To Moses Jeffres p. Acct.              16:16: 0              800
To Henry D. Hooe Clk. Overseers         5: 0: 0
To Robert Young for keeping Andrew Brown 6 Months and
    Burying him                                              500
To Peter Cotril for keeping Michael Killy & John
    Dunavin and Burying the former                           400
To Do. for keeping two poor persons 13 weeks at
12/ p. Week Assigned to J. Muschett     7:16: 0
To George Rainie p. Acct.               3: 5: 0
To James Muschett p. Acct.              1:16: 0
To Do. for Sundries furnished Andrew Oliver p. Order         200
To James Sissel & Wife two poor people                       800
To Elizabeth Lunceford a poor Woman                          300
To Rhoda Ellis for keeping Anne Binks one Month and
    Burying her                                              400
To Mary Peake a poor Woman                                   500
To Humphrey Calvert for keeping a Child 12 Mo.               600
To Susanna Barker a blind Woman                             1000
[150] To Elizabeth Forsithe for keeping a poor Child         600
To Charles Davis for keeping a poor Child                    600
To Elizabeth Reeds for keeping a poor Child                  600
To William Martin a poor Man                                 500
To Elijah Wood for keeping John Dunavin 3½ Mo.               300
To Colo. Jesse Ewell for Burying Wm. West a poor Man         300
To Do. for ½ a barl. of Corn furnished
    Elizabeth Bagnell a poor Woman      0: 8: 0
To Hannah Tingle for keeping her infirm Child                800
To Moses Robins for Sundry provisions
    furnished Isaac Murphy p. Acct.      2:12: 6
To Christian Highwarden a poor Woman to be paid to John
    Killy                                                    500
To Rheubin Dye for keeping John Pridmore 6 Months and
    Burying him                                              800
To Cuthbert Bullitt p. Acct.            2:10: 0
To Colo. Jesse Ewell for his assumpset
    for John Dunavin 1 Weeks Board      0: 6: 0
To Tobacco to pay the Cash Claimers                         5500
                                    £ 40: 9: 6             35300
To 6 p. Ct. on the above Sum of Tobo. is                    1918
                                                           37218
The fraction in the Sheriffs hands                          1638
                                                           38856
```

CONTRA   Cr.

By 3238 Tithables at 12 lb. Tobo. pr. poll is   38856

    Note there is a fraction in the Sheriffs hands due from last
year Amounting to 2878.
    Ordered that the Sheriff receive from each Tithable in this County
12 pounds of Tobacco to pay off the Different Claimers.
    [151] Ordered that Mr. Alexander Brown high Sheriff in Company
with Colo. William Alexander, Colo. Jesse Ewell and Mr. Bernard Hooe
or any two of them sell the Tobacco levied to pay the Cash Cliamers for
the best price that can be had.
    Signed, William Alexander, President; Jesse Ewell, James Grinstead,
James Gwatkin & John Kincheloe, Overs. Poor.

    [152] At a meeting of the Overseers of the Poor at Lewis Reno's
on the 28th day of October 1791
    Present: William Alexander, President; Colo. Jesse Ewell, Capt.
James Gwatkin, James Grinstead, Capt. Bernard Hooe & Capt. John
Kincheloe, Overseers of the Poor:

                  PRINCE WILLIAM COUNTY   Dr.

To Johnson Owings a Cripple   1200
To Richd. Shurley for keeping Wm. Shurley a blind Man 1000
To Robert Hamilton & Daughter two poor people   1200
To John Baze and his wife two poor People   1200
To Elisa. Doubty for keeping Elisabeth Wood an Idiot 600
To Clement Fare a poor Man   400
To John Casey a poor Man   1000
To Levina Crowson a poor Woman   600
To Isbel Forbis for keeping Ann Paris a poor Girl   1000
To Jacob Lannum for keeping his infirm Daughter   1000
To Anne Earls a poor Woman   600
To Sarah Williams for keeping Richd. Williams   400
To Mary Muckleberry a poor Woman   400
To Robert Hedges for keeping a poor Child   800
To Mary Turner a poor Woman   400
To Anne Williams a poor Woman   800
To Nancey Lunce for keeping Nancey Byrn   800
To Mary Posey a poor Woman   500
To John Cornhil & Wife two poor people   1000
To John Foxworthy for his Son   600
To William Annis for keeping a poor Child   800
To Ignatious Godwood for keeping an Idiot   800
To James Sissel and Wife two poor people   800
To Eliza. Lunceford a poor Woman   500
To Susanna Barker a poor Woman to be paid to James
   Grinstead   1000
To Mary Ann McMahon for keep'g a poor Girl   600

[153] To Elisabeth Forseythe for keep'g a poor Child		400
To Hannah Tingle for keeping a poor Child		800
To Lewis Reno for Burying Z. Potter		400
To Henry D. Hooe Clerk	5: 0: 0	
To Thomas Bristow for keep'g & Bury'g John Willow		520
To Vala. Barton for his son in Law a poor Man		1000
To Moses Jeffres p. Acct.		3225
To Stephen Pilcher for keeping Susanna Rigby		220
To Martha McAboy for keeping John Dunavin		200
To Caty Sergeant a poor Woman		500
To Joseph Stephens for keeping & Burying a poor Child		500
To Benja. Cooper for keep'g Elisabeth Smith 9 Months		900
To James Webster for keeping two poor Children		1200
To James Muschett p. Acct.		330
To Elisa. Doubty a poor Woman		400
To the Exrs. of William Carr p. Acct.	38: 4:10	
To Colo. Jesse Ewell p. Acct.	4: 2: 0	
To Capt. James Gwatkin p. Acct.	1:18: 1	
To William Chesshire a poor Man		600
To Capt. John Kincheloe p. Acct.	0:11: 0	
To a further allowance to Moses Jeffries		600
	£ 49:15:11	34625

Ordered that Colo. William Alexander and James Gwatkin make inquirey on what Terms a Piece of Land not exceeding two hundred Acres near the Centre of the County can be purchased for the Reception of the poor and report to the Next meeting.

Signed, William Alexander, Jesse Ewell, Bernard Hooe, James Gwatkin and James Grinstead, Oversrs. Poor.

[154]   At a meeting of the Overseers of the Poor on the 7th day of November 1791

Present: Colo. Jesse Ewell, Capt. Bernard Hooe, Capt. James Gwatkin and Mr. James Grinstead, Overseers of the Poor:

Brot. over the Amt. Levied on the 28th day of October 1791

In Cash and Tobacco	49:15:11	&	34625
To Jane Cole for keeping James McIntosh			400
To Tobacco Levied to pay the Cash Claimers			10000
			45025
To 6 p. ct. on the above Sum of 45025 pounds of Tobacco			2701
			47726
To a fraction in the Collectors hands			2814
			50540

CONTRA   Cr.

By 3610 Tithables at 14 lb. Tobacco p. poll   50540

Ordered that the Sheriff Collect from each Tithable in this County fourteen pounds of Tobacco.

Ordered that the Sheriff in Company with Colo. Jesse Ewell, Mr. Bernard Hooe and Capt. James Gwatkin or some one of them Sell the Tobacco levied to pay the Cash Claimers for the best price that can be had.

Signed, Jesse Ewell, Bernard Hooe, James Gwatkin & James Grinstead, Overseers of the Poor.

[155] At a meeting of the Overseers of the Poor at Gowen Adams's on the 28th of September 1792

Present: Thomas Lee, Thomas Harrison, Robert H. Hooe, William Helm and Philip Dawe, Overseers of the Poor:

Ordered that Thomas Lee be appointed President.
Ordered that Henry Dade Hooe be appointed Clerk.

PRINCE WILLIAM COUNTY	Dr. £ S d
To Richard Shurley for keep'g Wm. Shurley a blind Man	5: 0: 0
To Robert Hamilton and Daughter two poor people	6: 0: 0
To John Baize and his Wife two poor people	6: 0: 0
To Elisabeth Doubty for keep'g Elisabeth Wood an Idiot	5: 0: 0
To Clement Fare a poor Man	2: 0: 0
To John Casey a poor Man	5: 0: 0
To Livina Crowson a poor Woman	3: 0: 0
To Isbelle Forbis for keep'g Anne Paris a poor Woman	5: 0: 0
To Jacob Lannan for keep'g his infirm Daughter	5: 0: 0
To Anne Earls a poor Woman	3: 0: 0
To Sarah Williams for keep'g Richard Williams	2:10: 0
To Mary Muckleberry a poor Woman assigned to Mr. James Muschett	3: 0: 0
To Robert Hedges for keeping a poor Child	3: 0: 0
To Mary Turner a poor Woman	3: 0: 0
To Anne Williams a poor Woman	5: 0: 0
To George Barker for keeping Nancey Byrn for the present and insuing year	10: 0: 0
To Mary Posey a poor Woman	2:10: 0
To John Cornhill & his Wife two poor People	3: 0: 0
To John Foxworthy for keep'g his infirm Son	5: 0: 0
To Ignatius Godwood for keeping an Idiot	4: 0: 0
To Margret Sissel a poor Woman	3: 0: 0
To Elizabeth Lunceford a poor Woman	3:10: 0
To Susanna Barker a poor Woman to be paid to James Grinstead	5: 0: 0
To Mary Anne McMahon for keep'g a poor Girl	3: 0: 0
[156] To Hannah Tingle for keeping a poor Child	4: 0: 0
To Moses Jeffres p. Acct.	21:10: 0
To Caty Sergeant a poor Woman	2:10: 0
To James Grinstead for Burying Mary Peake	1:10: 0

To Richard Cole for keeping William Chesshire a poor
   Man 9 Months   5: 0: 0

To Richard Cole for keeping William Chesshire a poor Man 9 Months	5: 0: 0
To Jane Cole for keeping James McIntosh	3: 0: 0
To Dirk Greniore for himself and two Children	6: 0: 0
To Timothy King a poor Man assigned to Js. Muschett	2: 0: 0
To James Platt a poor Man	2: 0: 0
To James Williams a poor Man	6: 0: 0
To William Martin a poor Man	4: 0: 0
To John Ellis a poor Man	5: 0: 0
To James Muschett p. Acct.	1:10: 9
To William Smith pr. Acct.	0:10: 0
To James Espay pr. Acct.	0:15: 0
To Bernard Galligher pr. Acct.	1:12: 3
To Messrs. Lithgow & Lawson p. Acct.	0: 4: 0
To Philip Dawe for Mary Ellis a poor Woman	5: 0: 0
	£ 172:12: 0

Ordered that Mr. Thomas Harrison and William Helm inquire on what
terms a piece of Land can be purchased near the Centre of the County
for the Reception of the Poor and make report to the Next Meeting.
    Ordered that the Clk. advertise a Meeting of the Overseers of
the Poor at this place on the Second Monday in November next.
    Signed, Thomas Lee, Thomas Harrison, Robert H. Hooe, William
Helm, Philip Dawe.

    [157] At a Meeting of the Overseers of the Poor held at Adams
Tavern on the 12th day of November 1792
    Present: Thomas Lee, President; Edward Carter, Robert Howson
Hooe & Philip Dawe, Overseers of the Poor:

To amount Levied on the 28th day of September last	172:12: 0
To James Muschett pr. Acct.	3:11: 5
To Robert Hedges a further Allowance	1: 0: 0
To Isaac Hamrick for his infirm Son	3: 0: 0
To Thomas Chapman pr. Acct.	7:16: 0
To William Smith pr. Acct.	1: 2: 9
To William Annis for keeping two Children and Burying one	5: 0: 0
To George Weaver pr. Acct.	2: 0: 0
To John Hunter for Joe Nevil a poor Boy	5: 0: 0
To Ignatius Godwood a further Allowance	2: 0: 0
To James Fullum a poor Man	4: 0: 0
To John Hunter a poor Man	5: 0: 0
To Betty Stephens a poor Woman	5: 0: 0
To Philip Dawe pr. Acct.	0: 5: 3
To Priss Linett a poor Woman	3: 0: 0
To Charles Davis pr. Acct.	4:10: 0
To Moses Jeffres pr. Acct.	0: 7: 6
To John Simpson & Wife two poor People	6: 0: 0
To Colo. Jesse Ewell pr. Acct.	0: 9: 0
To Doctor William Graham pr. Acct.	18: 0: 0

To Anne Pate a poor Woman	5: 0: 0
To Morgan Williams a poor Man	5: 0: 0
To Mary Cusenberry pr. Acct.	2: 0: 0
To Mrs. Ford a poor Woman	3: 0: 0
To Henry Dade Hooe Clk.	5: 0: 0
To George Saffer pr. Acct.	1: 0: 0
[158] To Susanna Doyle pr. Acct.	1:13: 0
To James Webster for keep'g a poor Child	3: 0: 0
To Edward Harris a poor Man	5: 0: 0
To Jane Anderson for keeping Mary Neale	1: 4: 0
	£ 281:10:11

Adjourned tell tomorrow 10 Ocloke.

13th November 1792
Present: Thomas Lee, President; Edward Carter, Philip Dawe &
Robert H. Hooe, Overseers of the Poor:
Ordered that the high Sheriff pay to Yelverton Peyton on acct. of
his Claim in behalf of Betty Stephens and of his list of Delinquents
the Fractions of 1790 & 1791.

To Amount Brot. down	281:10:11
To the Contingent Fund	220: 0: 0
To 6 p. Ct. for Collecting	30: 1:10
	531:12: 9
To the Fraction remaining in the Collectors hand	13:18: 3
	545:11: 0

CONTRA   Cr.

By 3637 Tithables at 3/ pr. poll	545:11: 0

Ordered that the Sheriff receive from each Tithable in the County
three Shillings and pay off the different Claiments.
Ordered that the Sheriff pay off the Contingent Fund and Fraction
into the hands of Mr. Thomas Harrison and William Helm that they
in the first instances pay for the two Hundred Acres of Land Ordered
to be purchased for the use of the poor; that the same Gentlemen
contract for the Building a poor House Thirty Six feet by Twenty and
pay for the same out of [159] the Contingent Fund, and the Balle.
that may remain as soon as the Amount of these Applications can be
ascertained shall be by them equally Divided amongst the Overseers
of the Poor to be appropriated according to Law.
Ordered that the President get from Joseph Nevil an assignment
of his Claim agt. John B. Luckett and bring Suit for it so Reimburse
the County for Advances made him.
Signed, Thomas Lee, Edward Carter, Robert H. Hooe & Philip Dawe,
Overrs. Poor.

[160] At a Meeting of the Overseers of the Poor held in the Town
of Dumfriese on the 4th day of June 1793

Present: Thomas Lee, President; Thomas Harrison, Robert Howson Hooe and Philip Dawe, Overseers of the Poor:
Ordered that the Order made on the 13th of November 1792 Respecting the Building a poor House be rescinded and that the Gentlemen appointed to contract for the Building pursue the following plan to Wit: a framed House Sixteen Feet Square with a Stone or Brick Chimney Weather Boarded & Covered with Shingles and as many Logged Cabins as they may Judge Sufficient for the present, situated & built in Such Manner as they shall think best.
Signed, Thomas Lee Junr., Thomas Harrison, Robert H. Hooe & Philip Dawe.

[161] At a Meeting of the Overseers of the Poor at Gavan Adams Tavern on the 16th day of September 1793
Present: Thomas Lee, President; Thomas Harrison, William Helm and Philip Dawe, Overseers of the Poor:

PRINCE WILLIAM COUNTY	Dr.	£	S	d
To Richd. Shurley for Bury'g Wm. Shurley a poor Man		1:	0:	0
To Robert Hamilton & his Daughter two poor persons		6:	0:	0
To John Baize & his Wife two poor Persons		6:	0:	0
To Elisabeth Doubty for keeping Elisabeth Wood an Idiot		5:	0:	0
To Clement Fare a poor Man		2:	0:	0
To John Casey a poor Man		5:	0:	0
To Levina Crowson a poor Woman		3:	0:	0
To Isabelle Forbis for keep'g Ann Paris a poor Woman		5:	0:	0
To Jacob Lannum for keep'g his infirm Daughter		5:	0:	0
To Anne Earls a poor Woman		4:	6:	0
To Sarah Williams for keep'g Richd. Williams a Cripple		2:	10:	0
To Mary Muckleberry a poor Woman		3:	0:	0
To Anne Williams a poor Woman		5:	0:	0
To Mary Posey a poor Woman		2:	10:	0
To John Cornhill & Wife two poor Persons		3:	0:	0
To John Foxworthy for keep'g his infirm Son		5:	0:	0
To Margret Sissel a poor Woman		3:	0:	0
To Elisabeth Lunceford a poor Woman		3:	10:	0
To Ann McMahon a poor Girl		3:	0:	0
To Timothy King a poor Man		2:	0:	0
To James Platt a poor Man		2:	0:	0
To James Williams a poor Man		6:	0:	0
To William Martin a poor Man		6:	0:	0
To John Ellis a poor Man		5:	0:	0
To Moses Jeffres for keep'g two poor Persons		8:	0:	0
To Isaac Hamrick for keep'g his infirm Son		3:	0:	0
To William Annis for keep'g a poor Child		3:	10:	0
To James Fullum a poor Man		4:	0:	0

To Betty Stephens a poor Woman	5: 0: 0
[162] To John Simpson and Wife two poor Persons	6: 0: 0
To Anne Pate a poor Woman	5: 0: 0
To Old Granna Ford a poor Woman	3: 0: 0
To Edward Harris a poor Man	5: 0: 0
To Hannah Tingle for keep'g a poor Child	4: 0: 0
To James Grinstead for keep'g Susanna Barker a poor Person	7: 0: 0
To Philip Dawe for keep'g Mary Ellis a poor Woman	5: 0: 0
To Nancey Lunceford and two Poor Children	6: 0: 0
To Langhorne Dade Attorney at Law for Services	1: 8: 0
To William Lynn for keep'g Lewis Horsenail poor Man Eight Months	3:10: 0
To Amey Simonds a poor Woman	3: 0: 0
To Elisabeth Bryant a poor Woman	3: 0: 0
To Thomas Bobos for keep'g Cilia Wilkerson 7 Months	2:18: 0
To Do. for keep'g the Sd. Cilia Wilkerson the ensuing Year	5: 0: 0
To Ignatius Luckett & Wife two Poor Persons	10: 0: 0
To Walker Turner for Burying a poor Girl	1: 0: 0
To Jeremiah Danil for Burying Thos. Riley a poor Man	1: 0: 0
To Philip Dawe for keeping Mad Molly a poor Woman Six Weeks at Six Shillings pr. Week	1:16: 0
To Messrs. Steward & Muschett p. Acct.	8:15: 0
To Thomas Chapman p. Acct.	10: 6: 7
To Thomas Lee for furnishing Mrs. Rigby with two Barrels of Corn at 15/ per Barl.	1:10: 0
	£ 211:10: 7

Signed, Thomas Lee Jun.; Thomas Harrison, William Helm, Philip Dawe.

[163]   At a Meeting of the Overseers of the Poor at Mr. Smocks Tavern in the Town of Dumfries on Tuesday the 8 day of October 1793
    Present: Thomas Lee, President; Thomas Harrison, Philip Dawe and William Helm, Overseers of the Poor:

To Amount of Cash levied on the 16th of Sepr. last	211:10: 7
To Anne Moore a poor Woman	3: 0: 0
To Mary Hedges for keeping a poor Child	5: 0: 0
To James Grinstead for diging a Grave for a poor Woman	0: 3: 0
To Doctor George Rainey p. Acct.	2: 0: 0
To Ann Bunn a poor Woman	5: 0: 0
To George Beaver for Making 2 Coffins and Burying a poor Woman	2: 0: 0
To Thomas Chapman p. Acct.	0: 4: 4
To Saml. Ashton for keep'g Mary Neale a poor Woman	1:10: 0
To Mary Cusinberry for Burying a poor Woman	1: 0: 0
To Bernard Galligher pr. Acct.	0: 3: 6

To Cloe Hardin for keep'g Nancey Lunce and her Children
one Month   0:15: 1
To Messrs. Kirkbride & Shoemaker pr. Acct.   2:10: 0
To the high Sheriff for his list of Delinquents
given in by George Lane   21:19: 0
To Do. for a list of Delinquents given in by Wheeler   9:12: 0
To Moses Guy for Burying a poor Woman   0:10: 0
To Sarah Taylor for keeping 2 Children 2 Months   2: 0: 0
                                                            £ 268:17: 5

Adjourned till the 21st of this Month if fair, if not the next
fair day at Adams's Tavern.

Signed, Thomas Lee, Junr.; Thomas Harrison, William Helm & Philip
Dawe.

[164 and 165 blank, 166] At a Meeting of the Overseers of the
Poor a Gavan Adams's Tavern on the 21st of October 1793

Present: Thomas Lee, President; Thomas Harrison, William Helm
& Philip Dawe, Overseers of the Poor:

To Amt. of Cash levied and Brot. forward   268:17: 5
To Henry D. Hooe Clk. Overseers   5: 0: 0
To Thos. Boboe a further Allowance for keep'g Cielie
Wilkerson   10: 0
To the high Sheriff for a list of Delinquents given
in by William Allwell   8:13: 0
To John Hunter for keeping Rose Doudal 1 Month   1:10: 0
To John Matthews for Burying Caty Sergeant a
poor Woman   1: 0: 0
To Anne Godwood for Burying a poor Child   1: 0: 0
To John Hunter a poor Man   5: 0: 0
To the Contingent Fund   50:10: 0
To 6 pr. Ct. for the Collection of 342: 1: 4   21:16: 0
                                                            £ 363:18: 0

CONTRA   Cr.

By 3639 Tithables at 2/ p. Poll   £ 363:18: 0

Ordered that the Sheriff receive from each Tith. in the County
two Shillings and pay off the Different Claiments.

Ordered that the Sheriff pay the Contingent Fund to the President
of the Overseers of the Poor at the time appointed by Law.

Signed, Thomas Lee, Junr., Thomas Harrison, William Helm & Philip
Dawe.

[167] At a Meeting of the Overseers of the Poor held at Gavin
Adams's on the 13th of September 1794

Present: Thomas Lee, President; Thomas Harrison, Robert Howson
Hooe and Philip Dawe, Overseers of the Poor:

The public Creditors and Claiments Notified to Meet the Overseers of the Poor on the Second Saturday in October for Purposes therein expressed.

The Commissioners appointed to Contract for the Building the Poor Houses returned their A/c and proceedings to this day which is admitted and the Balance appearing to be due is Seven pounds one Shilling and two pence half penny independant of the last Contingent Fund.

On Motion made & Question being put, it is Resolved that no part of the Poor House lands be Rented.

Ordered that the President and the Reverend Thomas Harrison is Appointed a Committee to State a Set of Rules to Govern the Overseer of the Poor House & have them ready to present to the different applicants for that Office by the first Tuesday in next Month.

Adjourned to the second Saturday in October next.

Signed, Thomas Lee Junr., Thomas Harrison, Robert H. Hooe & Philip Dawe.

[168] At a Meeting of the Overseers of the Poor held at Gavin Adams's on the 8th day of November 1794 on various Adjournments

Present: Thomas Lee, President; Thomas Harrison, William Helm, Philip Dawe & Robert H. Hooe, Overseers of the Poor:

PRINCE WILLIAM COUNTY   Dr.

To Robert Graham Clk. for Certifying Randolphs Deed	...
To Richard Dounton pr. Acct.	...
To Alexander Jameson for Burying Wm. Ford	...
To Messrs. Henderson, Ferguson & Gibson pr. Acct.	...
To John Hunter for keeping Mad Molly	...
To William Smith pr. Acct.	...
To Messrs. Steward & Muschett pr. Acct.	...
To John Waters Junr. pr. Acct.	...
To Doctor George Leslie pr. Acct.	...
To Benjamin Reeve for Making a Coffin for Robert Hamilton a poor Man	...
To Howson Hooe Junr. pr. Acct.	...
To Basil Brawner pr. Acct.	...
To John Smith for keeping Elisabeth Forscythe	...
To Moses Jeffres pr. Acct.	...
To Robert H. Hooe for Ann Hamilton a poor Girl	...
To Mary Stone for keeping Nancey Moore a poor Child	...
To James Grinstead for keeping Susanna Barker	...
To Doctor John McDaniel pr. Acct.	...
To Henry D. Hooe Clk. Overseers of the Poor	...
To Philip Dawe pr. Acct.	...
	192:...

John Mathews is duly elected to Overlook the poor of this County and to be Subject to Such Directions as he may from time to time receive from the Overseers of the Poor and to enter into Bond etc.

for due performance of his duty to the President.

[169] Ordered that Philip Dawe give such directions for the Settling the Poor that may apply as he shall think fit and proper till the next Meeting and that the Said Meeting be held at Mr. Smocks Tavern in Dumfries on the 2d day of Next Court.

Signed, Thomas Lee Junr., Thomas Harrison, Philip Dawe, William Helm & Robert H. Hooe.

At a meeting of the Overseers of the Poor of Prince William County held in the Town of Dumfries on Tuesday the 2d day of Decr. 1794 by Adjournment

Present: Thomas Lee Jun., President; Thomas Harrison, William Helm & Philip Dawe, Overseers of the Poor of Said County:

	D. Ct.
To Thomas Chapman pr. Acct.	28.23

Ordered that Thomas Harrison lay in as much Corn and Pork as the Contingent Fund will Admit of and give such other Directions as he may judge necessary in having the Poor removed to the Poor houses and providing them with Necessary Cloathing and Beding and that a Commission of 2/2 pr. Ct. be allowed for his Trouble.

To Valentine Barton for Bury'g Morgan Williams a poor Man   3.33

Adjourned to Saturday the 13th of this Month to Meet at Gavin Adams's.

Signed, Thomas Lee Jun., Thomas Harrison, Philip Dawe & William Helm, Oversrs. Poor.

[170] At a Meeting of Overseers of the Poor held at Gavin Adams's on the 13th of December 1794 by Adjournment

Present: Thomas Lee, President; Robert H. Hooe, Philip Dawe and Thomas Harrison, Overseers of the Poor of Prince William County:

PRINCE WILLIAM COUNTY	Dr. D. Ct.
To Amount Brought Forward	223.6-
To Thomas Chapman pr. Acct.	3.5-
To Doctor John Spence pr. Acct.	71.3-
To Elisabeth Whitfield	6.8-

Ordered that the President be impowered and Authorised to Settle the Accts. that now Subsist between the late Sheriff and the County for the last two years which when Settled is to be returned to the Clk. and Committed to record.

To Thomas Fox for a levy over Charged & Cost	.7-
To Issabelle Forbis for keep'g Ann Parris a poor Girl	16.6-
To George Lane for a list of Delinquents	36.3-

To William Martin Junr. for Bording William Martin
    Senr. a poor Man 2 months   4.0-
To George Lane a Deputy Sheriff of Bernard Hooe Gent.
    high Sheriff produced and Settled an Acct. for the
    years 1792 and 1973 in part of the Poor Levies
    of said years.
To the Contingent Fund   841.2-
                                        1204.4-
To Six pr. Ct. for Collecting   76.8-
                                        1281.3-

CONTRA   Cr.

By 3844 Titheables at 2/ or 33 1/3 Cents ea.   1281.3-

    [171] Order'd that the sheriff receive from each Tithable in
this County two shillings or thirty three and one third Cents and
pay off the different Claiments.
    Order'd that the sheriff pay the Contingent Fund to the President
of the Overseers of the poor.
    Sign'd, Thos. Lee Senior, Thos. Harrison, Robert H. Hooe and
Philip Dawe.

    At a Meeting of the Overseers of the Poor held at Mr. Williams's
Tavern in Dumfries on the 4th day of June 1795
    Present: Thomas Lee, John McMillian, Alexander Bruce & Bernard
Hooe Junr., Overseers of the Poor:
    Thomas Lee Esqr. is appointed President of the Overseers of the
Poor.
    Henry D. Hooe is continued Clerk of the Overseers of the Poor.

PRINCE WILLIAM COUNTY   Dr. D. Cts.

To Humphrey Calvert pr. Acct.   5.0-
To Majr. Burr Peyton pr. Acct.   3.66

    The Overseers of the Poor then Adjourned to the 13th of this
Instant to Meet at the Poor Houses.
    Signed, Thomas Lee Senr., John McMillian, Alexander Bruce &
Bernard Hooe, Junr., Overseers.

    [172] At a Meeting of the Overseers of the Poor held at the
Poor Houses on the 10th day of July 1795 on various Adjournments
    Present: Thomas Lee Senr., President; Thomas Harrison, John
McMillian, Alexander Bruce and Bernard Hooe Junr., Overseers of the
Poor:
    Thomas Harrison Rendered an Acct. of his Receipts & Disbursments
of so much of the Various Contingent Funds as have (been) placed in
his Hands by which there appears to be due the Sd. Thomas Harrison
the Sum of Eighteen Pounds two Shillings & four pence 3 farthings.
    Ordered that the said Acct. be recorded & that the President pay

the above balance of Eighteen pounds two Shillins and four pence three farthings out of the Contingent Fund in his hands.

Ordered that the President pay Humphrey Calvert and Burr Peyton the Amt. of their Accts. Ordered to be Levied for them at the last Meeting.

Ordered that the President pay Thomas Davies his Acct. Rendered & Allowed.

Ordered that the President pay William Corwil his Acct. rendered & allowed.

Ordered that the President pay Richard Dounton his Acct. rendered & allowed.

Ordered that the President pay John Matthews his Acct. rendered & Received.

Ordered that the President pay James Grinstead his Acct. received & admitted.

Ordered that the President pay John Brewer his Acct. Rendered & admitted.

[173] Ordered that the President pay Anthony Lucas his Acct. rendered and Admitted.

The Overseers examined the Recipt and expenditures of Provisions and Order That the Overlooker Sell the Lard for the best price, also five hundred pounds of the Bacon. The overlooker to lay out the Amount of the Lard in Molasses for the use of the Poor and pay the Amount of the Bacon to the President.

The Accts. of the Overlooker to this date are examined & Admitted.

Ordered that the President pay the Overseers Wages.

The Overseers then Adjourned.

Thomas Lee Senr., Alexander Bruce, Thomas Harrison, John McMillian & Bernard Hooe Jun., Oversrs. Poor.

Dr.

The Overseers of the Poor to Thomas Harrison 1794	
To Acct. Rendered	212:18:10½
To pd. Weedon Smith 800 1b. Pork @ 32/	12:16
To pd. Do. Do. 251 1b. @ 36/	4:10: 4
To Paid Capt. Helm 1736 1b. @ 36/	31: 4:11½
To paid Joseph Brady 21 Barls. & 2 Bls. of Corn at 13/	13:18: 2
To Paid Donel Balce. Building the Poor Houses	18: 5: 0
To pd. by Mr. Muschett to Mr. Daw part of the Contingent Fund	12: 0: 0
To pd. Overseers Wages	8: 8: 0
To Cash pd. for 517 1b. Pork @ 30/	7:14: 1
[174] To Paid Hislop for 10 Barls. Corn at 11 Shillings	5:10: 0
To Commission	6:15: 3
	334: 0: 7 3/4
To Do. on 71 pounds	1:15: 6
	335:16: 1 3/4

-86-

                          1792 CONTRA   Cr.

By Contingent Fund   220: 0: 0
By Do. Do. for 1793   50;10;11
By Cash repaid by P. Dawe   6: 4: 8
By Cash paid by Geo. Lane   40:18: 2
To Balce. due p. Contra   317:13: 9
                                              ₺ 18: 2: 4 3/4

July 17th 1795 Recd. of Mr. Lee the Balce. of the Acct.

                                        Thos. Harison

        At a Meeting of the Overseers of the Poor the 17th day of October
1795 held at the Poor Houses
        Present: John McMillian, Philip Dawe, Alexander Bruce &
Bernard Hooe Junr.:
        Resolved that Nancy Lunce have notice this day that She is to
leave this place in one month from this date having behaved herself
in a disorderly Manner & it appearing to us she is able to get her
living having recovered her sight pretty well & is in good Health.
        Resolved that none of the People Recieved at the Poor Shall
leave the Place without Permission & that when they do they shall be
considered as discharged from it.
        [175] The Overlooker of the Poor is Ordered to purchase an Ax
for the use of the Different Houses & also to provide Tin Pans for
the use of the Poor as shall appear to him they Stand in need off.
        John McMillian, Philip Dawe, Alexander Bruce & Bernard Hooe Junr.

        At a Meeting of the Overseers of the Poor held at the Poor Houses
on the 12th day of December 1795
        Present: Thomas Lee, president; Thomas Harrison, John McMillian,
Philip Dawe & Bernard Hooe Junr., Overseers of the Poor.

                                                        D. Cts.

Ordered that the president pay to James Muschett   134.0
Ordered that the president pay to Danl. Carr   5.48
Ordered that the president pay to John Smith   16.75
Ordered that the president pay to Dr. Geo. Lesley   16.66
Ordered that the president pay to Timothy Brundige   2.25
Ordered that the president pay to Jno. Matthews   17.50
Ordered that the president pay to Mr. Thos. Harrison   10.0
Ordered that the president pay to Jno. Matthews   17.21
Ordered that the President pay to the Overseers of
    the Poor   11.0

        Ordered that the president purchase two thousand pounds of Pork
and Forty Barrels of Corn on the best terms he can, appropriating in
the first instance Fifty two pounds eight Shillings and four pence
the Balance in his hands of the last Contingent Fund.

Dr.

D. Cts.

To Samuel Wrye p. Acct.   4.0
To Thomas Chapman p. Acct.   15.42
To John Williams Clk.   0.44
To Henry D. Hooe Clk. Oversrs. Poor   16.66
To Daniel Carr p. Acct.   5.48
To Doniel Cole p. Acct.   5.0
To George Lane for his list of Delinquents rendered
  & examined   57.46

                                                               104.46

Ordered that John Matthews be Continued Overlooker at the Poor Houses the ensuing year at 25 pounds or 83 Dollars & 33 1/3 cents.

To the contingent Fund   783.27

                                                               887.73
To 6 p. Ct. on the above Sum   53.27

                                                               941.00

                        Contra   Cr.

By 3764 Titheables a 1/6 or 25 Cents   941.00

Ordered that each Titheable in the County pay to the Sheriff one Shilling & six pence or 25 Cents.
Ordered that the Sheriff pay the Contingent Fund put into his hands to collect to Alexander Bruce agreeable to Law.
The Clerk is Ordered not to Deliver a list of the County Claims to the Sheriff tell he has entered into Bond wth. the President for the Faithful Performance of his duty.
Ordered that Philip Dawe furnish such Cloths & other Necessaries as are wanted for the use of the Poor for the President and ensuing year on the best terms he can on a Credit.
Thos. Lee Senr., John McMillian, Philip Dawe, Thos. Harrison & Bernard Hooe Junr., Oversrs. Poor.

[177] At a meeting of the Overseers of the poor held at the poor Houses the 30th day of April 1796
Present: Thos. Harrison, John McMillion, Alexander Bruce & Philip Dawe, Overseers of the Poor:

From the proceeds of Jones's Donation Prince W. County   Cr.

By the Revd. Thos. Harrisons a/c Dollars & Cents   25.49
" Philip Dawes a/c   52.92
" Alexander Bruce a/c   25.49
" John McMillions a/c   7.
By a balce. from Wm. Helm a former Overseer   9.11

                                                               120.01

Having this day recd. a letter from Mr. John Pope enclosing the sum of Five Pounds twelve shillings which sum he wishes may be apply'd to the education of poor Children in the same manner as Jones's Donation which sum is day lodged in the hand of Mr. Thos. Harrison.

Mr. Alexander Bruce is empower'd to pay to Issabelle Forbes for the Keeping Ann Parish what is now due her agreeable to the time for which she has not been paid out of the money that may hereafter be lodg'd in his hands of the Contingent funds. he will also pay Ignatius Ransome for Keeping & burying John Carey agreeable to time & his making affidavit to his a/c out of the aforesaid funds.

Its agreed by the board that Philip Dawe may take in consideration the situation of Hannah Tingle and assist if necessary.

PRINCE WILLIAM COUNTY Dr.

To James Keys for Carrying rails per a/c Dollars & Cents	4.0
" Daniel Cole for find'g plank & nails & mak'g a Coffin	2.50
" John Matthews overlooker per a/c	3.55
" Thos. Harrison for removing Nancy Luncef'd to the Poor Houses	1.0
	11.95

The description of the several poor persons now at the poor Houses as hereafter mention'd Viz.:

William Miliner deaf and a very old man
[178] James Wilky a very deaf old man
William Martin deaf and blind
Celia Wilkinson very infirm
Ann Lunceford and Child said Ann Lunceford to W...
Arrabelle Baze a blind troublesome old Woman
Elizabeth Wood an insane Woman
Elisabeth Doughty to Assist in Washing.

Thomas Harrison, John McMillion, Philip Dawe and Alexander Bruce, Overseers Poor.

[179] At a Meeting of the Overseers of the Poor held at the Poor House on the 27th day of August 1796
Present: the Revd. Thomas Harrison, John McMillian, Alexander Bruce, Philip Dawe, Bernard Hooe Junr., Overseers of the Poor:
James Wigginton a Deputy Sheriff having produced a list of Delinquents for the year 1794 which is examined and Allowed Amounting

D.Cts.
to   61.75

Ordered that Mr. Alexander Bruce employ some person to Convey Ann Parris a Poor Girl from the House of Issabell Forbis to the Poor Houses and that the Overlooker receive her under his care.

Ordered that the Former Overseers of the Poor who have not Settled their Accts. relative to Jones's Donation be notified to Meet at

Dumfries the first day of October Court next for that purpose.

The Overseers of the Poor then adjourned till the first Day of October Court next then to be convened at Mrs. Williams Tavern in Dumfries at three Oclock past Meridian.

Signed, John McMillian, Thomas Harrison, Philip Dawe, Bernard Hooe Junr. & Alexander Bruce, Oversrs. of the Poor.

[180]   At a Meeting of the Overseers of the Poor held at Mr. Mitchels Tavern in Dumfries the 7th day of November 1796

Present: Thomas Lee, President; John McMillion, Alexander Bruce, Philip Dawe & Thomas Harrison, Overseers of the Poor:

	Dr.
Prince William County	D.Ct.
To Samuel Cornwil p. Acct.	11.55

Ordered that John Matthews be continued Overlooker of the Poor at the Poor Houses the ensuing year he giving Bond & Security to the President on principles this day agreed on.

Signed, Thomas Lee Senr., John McMillion, Alexander Bruce, Thomas Harrison & Philip Dawe.

[181] At a Meeting of the Overseers of the Poor Summoned & held at the Poor House of Prince William County the Ninth day of December 1796

Present: Thomas Lee, President; Thomas Harrison, John McMillian, Alexander Bruce & Philip Dawe, Overseers of the Poor:

Prince William County	Dr.
	D. Ct.

James Wigginton a Deputy Sheriff for the Sd. County having produced a list of Delinquents for the year 1795 which is examined and allowed amounting to   41.0

George Lane being also another Deputy Sheriff having produced another list of Delinquents which is also examined and allowed for the year 1975 Amounting to   40.25

An application being made to the Overseers of the Poor by William Ashby to have his infant child received and Supported at the Charge of the County and being put to the Vote the Majority was opposed to it. Mr. Harrison Voted for the acception of the Child and advocated it vehemently.

George Lane having presented his Acct. with County & being found right is admitted.

James Wigginton having presented his Acct. with the County and being examined found right is also admitted.

To Henry D. Hooe Clk. Oversrs. of the Poor   20.0

Ordered that each Titheable pay the Sheriff one Shilling or Seventeen Cents being the Amount of the next Levy.

[182] To the Contingent Fund   600.27
To Six p. Ct. for Collecting   39.61
                                                                660.28

                              Contra   Cr.

By 3884 Tithables at 17 Cents p. pol   660.28

    Signed, Thomas Lee Senr., Thomas Harrison, Alexr. Bruce, John
McMillian & Philip Dawe, Oversrs. Poor.

    [183] At a Meeting of the Overseers of the Poor held at the Poor
Houses of prince William County on the 8th day of December 1797
    Present: Thomas Lee, President; John McMillian, Thomas Harrison
and Bernard Hooe Junr., Overseers of the Poor:
    Ordered that the former and present Overseers of the Poor be
called on for a Statement of their application of Jones's Donation
& that they be requested to make it to the Clerk of the Overseers
to be laid before their Special Meeting for the purpose.
    Ordered that the present Overseers of the Poor be Notified to
attend at the Poor Houses the Second Friday in January or the first
fair day thereafter if it should prove not fair and that the Clerk
Notify the Absentees of the present Meeting.
    Ordered that this day Week the Overseers of the Poor Meet at the
Poor Houses for their ordinary Business and that the Absentees to
this Meeting be Notified by the Clerk.
    Ordered that John Matthews be continued Overlooker on the same
terms at the poor Houses as for the last year.
    Signed, Thomas Lee, p.O.P.; Thomas Harrison, John McMillian &
Bernard Hooe Junr.

    [184] At a Meeting of the Overseers of the Poor for the County
of Prince William in the Town of Dumfries at the House of George
Williams on the 5th day of January and at the Poor Houses on the 2d
Friday in January and on the 2 day of February 1798 by appointment
    Present: Thomas Harrison, Philip Dawe, John McMillion and
Bernard Hooe, Overseers of the Poor:
    Ordered that five pounds out of the contingent Fund be paid to
John Foxworthy for the Maintenance & Suppor of his Son a Fittified
Child.
    Ordered that the Sum of Five pounds be paid out of the contingent
Fund to Hannah Tingle for the Maintence and Support of her Son an
Idiot.
    Ordered that the Sum of eight pounds nine & six pence be paid to
Doctor Spence for Attendance and Medicine furnished the poor out of
the Contingent Fund.
    Ordered that one pound four Shillings be paid to the Executors of
Danl. Cole Deceased for two Coffins furnished the Poor out of the
Contingent Fund.
    Ordered that the Sum of one pound ten shillings be allowed &
paid to Rody Blancett for Burying William Scott a poor Man out of the

Contingent Fund.

Ordered that next Saturday or the next fair day be appointed for a Meeting of the Overseers of the Poor and that John Matthews the Overlooker give Notice personally to the absent Overseers that they are to Meet at the Poor Houses on Sd. day.

Signed, Thomas Harrison, Philip Dawe, John McMillian & Bernard Hooe Junr.

[185] At a Meeting of the Overseers of the Poor held at the Poor Houses on February the 10th day 1798

Present: Thomas Harrison, Philip Dawe, John McMillian, Alexander Bruce & Bernard Hooe, Overseers of the Poor:

Ordered that the first Monday in March next be Appointed for a Meeting of the Overseers of the Poor at George Williams's Tavern in the Town of Dumfries and that Colo. Lee President have Notice in the meantime that he be prepared with his Acct. to Settle the Contingint. Fund placed in his hands for the year 1793 which appears unsettled.

Ordered that John Matthews Overlooker give Colo. Lee Notice of the Foregoing Order.

Ordered that Mr. Bruce pay John Williams two Dollars & 29 Cents for Recording Randolphs Deed....

Ordered that Mr. Bruce pay Cloe Hay thirty Shillings for Keeping Ashbys Child one Month & Burying it.

Ordered that Alexander Bruce pay John McMillan his Acct. Amount Ten Pounds twelve Shillings & 3 pence.

Ordered that it be entered on record that Philip Dawe has Settled his Acct. with the Overseers for a part of the Contingent Fund put into his hands by Alexander Bruce Amounting to ten pounds eighteen Shillings and two pence.

Ordered that Mr. Bruces Accts. & Settlement of his Accompts for two years rects. & Expenditures be Admitted to record as a final Settlement with the Overseers of the Poor.

Ordered that each Tithable pay twenty one Cents in Prince William County for the year 1797 & that the Sheriff be empowered to Collect the Same after giving Bond & Security to the President of the [186] Overseer of the Poor for the said County amounting to Eight hundred & twenty four dollars & Sixty seven Cents.

D.Ct.

By 3927 Tithables at 21 Cents	824.67
6 p. Ct. for the collection is	49.48
	775.19

Ordered that George Lane be paid for Delinquencies for the year 1796   26.5

Ordered that James Wigginton be paid for Delinquencies for the year 1796 to be Collected out of the Contingent Fund   30.5

Ordered that the Sheriff of Prince William County pay the above Sum of eight hundred and twenty four Dollars & 67 Cents after

Deducting Six per Ct. for the Collection to the Overseers of the Poor for the time being for their appointment and Direction.

Ordered that Nancy Lunce be continued one Month longer in order to provide herself some other support different from that of a pensioner and from that time she be dismissed.

Ordered that John Matthews be paid his Acct. amounting to ten Dollars & Seventeen Cents out of the Contingent Fund for Services rendered by his Wife at the Poor Houses.

Signed, Thomas Harrison, Alexr. Bruce, John McMillian, Bernard Hooe Junr., Philip Dawe.

[187] At a Meeting of the Overseers of the Poor for the County of Prince William at the Poor Houses on the 29th day of March 1798

Present: Thomas Lee Senr., Thomas Harrison, Philip Dawe, John McMillian & Alexander Bruce, Overseers of the Poor:

Ordered that Thomas Lee Senr. pay to the Overseers of the Poor to be appointed for the ensuing year the Sum of two pounds forteen Shillings & five pence balance due of the Contingent Fund which was under his Management.

Ordered that the present & the Overseers of the Poor Preceeding Settle their receipts of Jones's Donation with the Revd. Mr. Harrison and after paying the Claims against them pay the balance into Mr. Harrisons hands who is to let the same out to Interest to Mr. William Helm on a distrainable Mortgage for the Security of the Principal & punctual payment of the Annual Interest or any other person Mr. Helms declining to take it.

Ordered that the Revd. Thomas Harrison call on Mr. Thomas S. Bullitt for Jones's Donation lent to the late Honble. Cuthbert Bullitt and if Mr. Thos. S. Bullitt chooses to renew his Bond on the present Legal Interest and Same Security to let him have it, or put it out to Interest to some other person on the same terms.

Ordered that the Sheriff pay to Stewart & Muchsett their Acct. of 1797 & 1798 Amounting to three pounds eighteen Shillings out of the Contingent Fund now Collecting.

[188] Ordered that the Sheriff pay to Robert Howson Hooe twelve Shillings due him p. Acct. out of the Contingent Fund now Collecting.

Ordered that the Sheriff pay Thomas Harrison three Dollars, Philip Dawe three Dollars, John McMillian three Dollars, Alexander Bruce three Dollars & Thomas Lee Senr. three Dollars out of the Contingent Fund.

Signed, Thomas Lee Senr., Thomas Harrison, Philip Dawe, John McMillian, Alexander Bruce.

At a Meeting of the Overseers of the Poor of Prince William County Summoned & held at the Poor House of the Said County on the 29th day of September 1798

Present: Thomas Lee, Thomas Harrison, John McMillian, Philip Dawe & Alexander Bruce, Overseers of the Poor:

Thomas Lee is Elected President of the Overseers of the Poor.

Henry Dade Hooe is Elected Clerk of the Overseers of the Poor.

Thomas Harrison is Elected & appointed Treasurer for the ensuing year and that the Sheriff pay the present Contingent Fund into his hands after Deducting therefrom appropriations heretofore made where [189] The Sheriff may have already Complied with them.

Signed, Thomas Lee Senr., Thomas Harrison, Philip Dawe, John McMillian, Alexander Bruce.

Ordered that Thomas Lee be added to the Order of the 29th of March last respecting Jones's Donation and that they bring the Business to a Conclusion as Spedily as possible and make report to the Overseers of the Poor.

Ordered that the Revd. Thomas Harrison add the Money lodged by Mr. Pope to that part of Jones's Donation to be Loaned to William Helm.

Then adjourned to Friday 26th Octobr. next.

Signed, Thomas Lee Senr., Thomas Harrison, John McMillian, Alexr. Bruce & Philip Dawe.

At a Meeting of the Overseers of the Poor held at the Poor Houses on the 26th of October 1798

Present: Thomas Harrison, John McMillian, Philip Dawe and Gerard Alexander, Overseers of the Poor:

Ordered that the Collectors of the Poor rate Levy be Called on to produce their Books and Accompts at the next Meeting of the Overseers of the Poor and account for all Monies Collected from the Delinquents heretofore rendered.

The Clerk is hereby ordered not to give a list of the County Claims and the proceeding of the Overseers of the Poor to their Collector till he has entered into Bond with Sufficient [190] Security for his Faithful performance with the President of the Overseers of the Poor.

Ordered that Henry Dade Hooe settle the Accts. of Issabelle Forbis and make report to the Next Meeting of the Overseers of the Poor.

Ordered that each Tithable person pay the collector of the Poor Rate Levy Twenty one Cents amounting to: 823.20
and that he be allowed 6 p. Ct. which is   49.39
By 3920 Tiths. at 21 Cents   823.20
         773.81

Ordered that the Collector pay the above Sum of Seven hundred and Seventy three Dollars and eighty one Cents to the Treasurer of the Overseers of the Poor.

Signed, Thomas Harrison, John McMillian, Philip Dawe & Gerard Alexander.

At a Meeting of the Overseers of the Poor in the Town of Dumfries on Monday the 5th day of November 1798

Present: Thomas Lee, John McMillian, Philip Dawe, Gerard Alexander Junr. & Thomas Harrison:

Ordered that John Matthews be continued Manager at the Poor Houses for the ensuing year on the same Wages as he has received this present year and that he give Bond & Security for the faithful performance of his duty to the President.

[191] Ordered that the Treasurer pay to Messrs. Steward &
Muschett their Acct. of ₤ 16:14: 8.
Ordered that the Treasurer pay to William Hammel Thirty Shillings
for Burying Presley Anderson and the Necessary Furnitures.
Ordered that the Treasurer pay Thomas Harrison Six Dollars,
Philip Dawe Five Dollars, John McMillian Six Dollars, Thomas Lee four
Dollars & Gerard Alexander two Dollars for their Services to this
date.
Signed, Thomas Lee Senr., Thomas Harrison, Philip Dawe, John
McMillian & Gerard Alexander.

[192] At a meeting of the Overseers of the Poor held at the
Poor House of Prince William County on the 15 day of November 1799
by Adjournment
Present: Thomas Harrison, John McMillian, Philip Dawe & Gerard
Alexander, Overseers of the Poor:

Prince William County	Dr.
To Doctor Bronaugh p. Acct.	35.
To Doctor John Spence p. Acct.	36.
To Jane Smith p. Acct.	16.
To Alexander Jamison for Making a Coffin for a poor Woman	2.
To John Burroughs for Keeping Joseph Lunce four Months	6.
To Charles Butler for Making a Coffin for Tingles Son to be pd. to George Lane	2.
To Ignatious Mitchell for burying and Nursing a poor Boy	4

Ordered that the Sheriff Summon Philip Harrison, Basil Taylor,
Thomas Harrison and Ann Benson to Prove a Mortgage from William
Helm to the Overseers of the Poor.

To James Wiginton a Deputy Sheriff for his list of Delinquents for the year 1797 and 1798	60.
To George Lane a Deputy Sheriff in the Lower District for a list of Delinquents for the year 1797 & 1798	75.
To John Matthews for extraordinary Services p. acct. Rendered	32.7
To John Foxworthy for his infirm Son	20.0

The Reverend Thomas Harrison having this day presented his Acct.
to the Bord and being examined is found right and the Balance
Sixteen Dollars and fifty nine Cents is due the County, Ordered
that it be recorded.

[193] Ordered that each Titheable Person pay the Collector 25
Cents Amounting to   998.00
6 p. Cent on the above Sum is   59.88
                                                            ───────
                                                            938.12
     Ordered that George Lane be Appointed to Collect the Poor Rate
Levy after giving Bond and Security to the Overseers of the Poor for
the faithful Performance of his duty.
     Ordered that Mr. Thomas Harrison be Appointed Treasurer and that
he Settle and receive from the Collector the above Sum of 998
Dollars after Deducting therefrom his Commission and Delinquents.
     Ordered that John Matthews be continued Overlooker on the same
terms as heretofore.
     Ordered that the Treasurer pay each Member that has Attended at
this Meeting one Dollar.
     John McMillian, Philip Dawe, Thomas Harrison, Gerard Alexander.

     [194 blank, 195] At a Meeting of the Overseers of the Poor by
Adjournment on the 16th day of Octobr. 1800 at the Poor Houses
     Present: Thomas Harrison, Philip Dawe, John McMillian & Gerard
Alexander:
     The Accts. of the Revd. Thomas Harrison (Treasurer of the Poor
contingent Fund) being laid before the Board and found to be correct
It appears that the Balance due by the Sd. Treasurer as p. the Accts.
Stated is 37.5.
     Ordered that the Treasurer pay Jno. Matthews Overlooker of the
Poor ₺ 25 for his Services at the Poor Houses for the year
1800   83.34
     Ordered that Mr. Matthews be allowed for Nursing an Orphan for Twelve
Months Last past Twenty Dollars   20.00
     Ordered that the Poor rate for the year 1801 be paid at 17 Cents
p. Tithe and that the Collector demand that Sum of each Titheable
Amounting in the Whole to 650.8   650.08
6 p. Cent for Collection is   39.00
                                                            ───────
                                                            611.08
     Ordered that the Collector enter into Bond wth. Security for the
faithful Performance of his Collection to the President of the
Overseers of the Poor previous to entering on his duty.
     Ordered that the Overseers of the Poor do Meet at the Poor Houses
on the 7 of November if fair if not the Next fair day and that Mr.
Matthews notify the absent Overseers of the time.
     Ordered that George Lane the Collector of the Poor rates last year
attend the Bord of Overseers on the 7th of Novr. and render to the
Bord an Acct. of his Collection & that Mr. Matthews notify him to that
effect.
     Signed, Thomas Harrison, Philip Dawe, John McMillian & Gerard
Alexander.

     [196] At a meeting of the Overseers of the Poor held at the
Poor Houses on the 7th day of November 1800
     Present: Thomas Lee, President; Thomas Harrison, John McMillian
& Gerard Alexander:

To Moses Moss p. Acct. to be pd. by the Treasurer 16
James Wigginton a Deputy Sheriff for the Sd. County
 having Presented his list of Delinquints for the
 year 1799 and being examined it is Ordered that
 the Treasurer pay him   62.2
George Lane a Deputy Sheriff in the lower District
 of Sd. County having also presented his list of
 Delinquents for the year 1799 being examined it
 is Ordered that the Treasurer pay him 38.5
Ordered that the Treasurer pay Jesse Murphey two
 Dollars & Fifty Cents first deducting therefrom
 the Amt. of his Levy for Last year being Twenty
 five Cents to be pd. to D. Sheriff Wigginton 2.5

  Ordered that John Matthews be continued Overlooker at the Poor
Houses for the ensuing year and that he be allowed Twenty pounds
with the other usual allowances for his Services and that he enter
into Bond with the President for the Faithful Performance of his
duty.
  Mr. Thomas Harrison & Mr. John McMillian dissents to the above Order.

Amount of Donation due for 1799 ₺ 44: 5: 0
Amount of Appropriations made by the Overseers of
 the Poor out of Jones's Donation p. Accts.
 rendered 41:19: 8
Balance in the Treasurer Mr. Harrisons hands Received
 from Mr. Bullitts Executor 2: 5: 4
            ₺ 44: 5: 0

  Ordered that the Treasurer pay to Elisabeth Harrison Six Dollars
& fifty Cents for attending Molly Barrett during her Illness and
Such other Sum as he shall think Reasonable for Moving her to the
Poor House.
  [197] An Order having been made by the Overseers of the Poor at
their Meeting on the 29th of March 1798 that the Revd. Thomas
Harrison call on Mr. Thos. S. Bullitt (as p. Order) and they being
informed of Mr. Bullitts objection Ordered that Mr. Gerard Alexander
and Mr. Thomas Lee examine the Deed of Mortgage for the Money
loaned and take such steps as they may Judge best to have their
former Order carried into effect.
  Ordered that the Clk. in future deliver to each person a Copy of
Orders made by the Overseers of the Poor where they are interested.
  Ordered that the Treasurer pay to Henry D. Hooe his Wages, Viz.,
Twenty Dollars for Acct'g as Clk. to the Overseers.
  Ordered that the Treasurer collect from Capt. Helm the Interest
due for the Money Loaned of Jones's Donation and hold it Subject to
future appropriations.
  Ordered that John Brown high Sheriff be Collector of the Levy for
the ensuing year he giving Bond & Security to the President for his

faithful Performance.

Signed, Thomas Lee Sr., Thomas Harrison, John McMillian, Gerard Alexander.

[198]   At a Meeting of the Overseers of the Poor Summoned & held at the Poor House of Prince William County on the 19th day of September 1801

Present: Thomas Lee, Philip Dawe and Alexander Bruce. There not being a quorum to proceed to Business it is Ordered that the Meeting be adjourned to Friday the 9th of October if fair if not the next fair day.

Signed, Thomas Lee Sr., Philip Dawe, Alexr. Bruce.

At a Meeting of the Overseers of the Poor of Prince William County held at the Poor House on the 9th day of October 1801 by appointment

Present: Thomas Harrison, John McMillian & Philip Dawe, and there not being a quorum to proceed to Business it is again Ordered that the Meeting be adjourned to Saturday the 24th of the present Month at George Williams's Tavern in Dumfries and that Mr. Matthews Notify the absent Members of the time & place of Meeting.

Signed, Thomas Harrison, Philip Dawe, John McMillian.

At a Meeting of the Overseers of the Poor called & held ... Dumfries by appointement on the 24th of October 1801

Present: Thomas Lee, John McMillian, Thomas Harrison, Philip Dawe & Gerard Alexander:

Thomas Lee Esqr. is unanimously Elected & appointed President, Mr. Thomas Harrison Treasurer & Henry D. Hooe Clerk of the Overseers of the Poor.

	Dr.
Prince William County	$

Ordered that William Shaw be Allowed for his list of Delinquents for the year 1800 the Sum of ten Dollrs 3 Cents	10.03
Ordered that William Renoe be Allowed for his list of Delinquents for 1800 Amounting to	11.
Ordered that Francis Johnson be Allowed for his list of Delinquents for 1800 Amounting to	29.
Ordered that the Treasurer pay William Carter p. Acct.	5.
[199] Present: Mr. Alexander Bruce:	
Ordered that the Treasurer pay to Philip Dawe pr. Acct.	19.25
Ordered that the Treasurer pay to John Cooke for Burying Robert Bryson a poor Man	5.
Ordered that the Treasurer pay Bernard Ghalligher the Amount of his Acct. which is	10.30
Ordered that the Treasurer pay William Smith the Amount of his Acct. which is	4.

Ordered that the Treasurer pay to Philip Dawe p. his
    Acct. rendered   3.28
Ordered that the Treasurer pay John McMillian for
    his Attendance   1.0
Ordered that the Treasurer pay Gerard Alexander
    one dollar & Mr. Bruce Three for their Attendance   4.0
Ordered that the Treasurer pay to Colo. Lee two
    Dollars and Receive one Dollar himself for their
    Services   3.
                                                  105.15

	Contra	Cr.
By 3856 Titheables at Ninteen Cents each		732.64
To 6 p. Cent for the Collection		43.95
		688.69
		732.64

    Ordered that each Titheable pay the Collector Ninteen Cents.
    Ordered that the Sheriff of the County be collector and that he
pay the Treasurer the above Sum of Seven hundred and thirty Two
Dollars & Sixty four Cents after deduct'g therefrom his Commission
for Collecting having previously given Bond & Security to the
Treasurer for Said Collection.
    The Reverend Thomas Harrison Treasurer having presented his
Accts. with the Overseers of the Poor from November 1800 to this
date Amounting to Seven hundred eighty three Dollars & twenty one
Cents is examined & Allowed by which Sd. Acct. there remains in
his hands a Balance of two hundred and fourteen Dollars & seventy
nine Cents of the Collection of 1800.
    [200] Ordered that the Treasurer furnish for John Foxworth a
Suit of Course Cloths & two Shirts for his infirm Son a poor boy.
    Ordered that John Matthews be continued Overlooker at the poor
House the ensuing year on the Same terms as heretofore & under the
Same Restrictions.
    Application having been made to the Board by William Evans &
John Jones, Ordered that they be admitted at the Poor Houses if they
choose to receive the Benefit of the Institution.
    Ordered that the Meeting be Adjourned to the first Friday in
November being the Sixth day of the Month if fair if not the next
fair day.
    Signed, Thomas Lee, Thos. Harrison, Alexr. Bruce, Gerard
Alexander, John McMillian, Philip Dawe.

    At a Meeting of the Overseers of the Poor held by Appointment
at the Poor House of Prince William County on the Sixth day of
November 1801
    Present: Thomas Harrison, John McMillian & Gerard Alexander,
Overseers of the Poor:
    There not being a quorum the Meeting is adjourned to the last
Monday in this Month.

Signed, John McMillian, Thos. Harrison & Gerard Alexander.

[201] At a Meet'g of the Overseers of the Poor called & held
at the Poor House of Prince William County on the 13th Novr. 1802
    Present: John McMillian, Thomas Harrison, Gerard Alexander &
Philip Dawe, Overseers of the Poor:
    The Revd. Mr. Thomas Harrison having presented his Acct. with
the Overseers and being examined found right amounting to five
hundred & one Dollars forty two Cents and there appears a balance
due from him to the County amounting to one hundred & forty eight
Dollars & Sixty Six Cents on the receipts of the year 1800.

		Dr.
	Prince William Coty.	D.Cts.
Ordered that George Chapman a Deputy Sheriff in one of the uper districts be Allowed for his list of Delinquents for the year 1801		11.78
Ordered that William Shaw a Deputy in the other district above the Runs be allowed for his list of Delinquents for the year 1801		12.16
Ordered that John Linton Do. be allowed for his list of Delinquents in the Lower District for the year 1801		32.87
Ordered that the Treasurer pay John Foxworthy the Sum Six Dollars & Sixty Six Cents for the Clothing of his infirm Son		6.66
Ordered that the Treasurer pay John Matthews Sixty Six Dollars & Sixty Six Cents due for his Services as Overlooker at the Poor House for the year 1801		66.66
Ordered that the Sheriff receive from each Tithe twelve and a half Cents he having previously entered into Bond with the President for the Faithful of his duty amounting to		491.87
To 6 p. Ct. Commission for Collecting		29.51
		462.36

	Contra	Credit
By 3935 Titheables at 12½ Cents		491.87

[202] Ordered that the Collector pay to the Treasurer the above
Sum of four hundred Ninty one Dollars and eighty Seven Cents after
deducting Twenty Nine Dollars & Fifty one Cents his Commission for
Collecting.
    The Overseers then adjourned to Thursday next the 18th of the
Month if fair if not the next fair day.
    Signed, Thomas Harrison, John McMillian, Philip Dawe & Gerald
Alexander.

At a Meet'g of the Overseers of the Poor held by appointment on 18th day of November 1802

On Application from Adam Douglas to pay him for keeping an Orphan Child which by Order of Court was directed to be bound to him & which he refused to acquiese to, Ordered that the said application be rejected.

Ordered that the Treasurer pay Issabelle Forbis the Sum of Four pounds Six Shillings & eight pence in Dollars & Cents is fourteen Dollars & forty two Cents p. Acct. Settled & Filed.

John Foxworthy having Petitioned for a Maintainance for his Son an infirm young Man the Petition is rejected on the General Principle that no person in future may apply other than to enter at the poor House.

Ordered that Mr. Thomas Harrison be continued Treasurer for the Ensuing year.

Ordered that the Acct. Settled this day with the commissioners under the Act of General Assembly for the sale of the Gleebe Land be recorded.

Ordered that Gerard Alexander & John McMillian ... the amount of the Said Sales being three hundred & ... one pounds Sixteen Shillings & three pence which is Dollars & Cents Eleven hundred and Six Dollars and four cents to Mr. James Muschett Mercht. in Dumfries on the same terms of the Money Loaned of Jones's Donation with Alteration of the principle being Subject to the call of the Overseers of the Poor on giving the Sd. Muschett ... Months previous Notice. The Sd. Muschett to give as Security a Mortgage on his lands in the County of Prince William near the Red House which Sd. Sum the Sd. John McMillian acknowledges the rect. of.

[203] Ordered that John McMillian or Gerard Alexander settle the Acct. of Receipts & expenditures of Interest due from Jones's Donation with Mr. Thomas Harrison.

Ordered that John Matthews be continued Overlooker for the Ensuing year on the same terms as for the present and under the same restriction.

Ordered that the Treasurer pay Thomas Anderson one dollar for Bringing John Jones a poor Man to the Poor House.

Ordered that the Treasurer pay to John Matthews twenty eight Dollars & Sixty Six Cent p. Acct.

Ordered that the Treasurer pay Henry D. Hooe twenty Dollars for his Services as Clk. to the Overseers of the Poor & that the payment made of Twenty Dollars by the Treasurer on the 20th day of August last to the Sd. Hooe be confirmed it being for his Services for the year 1801.

John Matthews Overlooker at the Poor Houses having presented his Acct. which examined found right & passed.

Ordered that the Treasurer pay John Matthews Sixty Six Dollars and Sixty Six Cents for his Services for the year 1802.

Ordered that the County Surveyer proceed to carry into effect the entry made by Colo. Lee on the 27th day of October last & that the Treasurer pay the Legal fees & the business being ended the Overseers Adjourned.

Signed, Thomas Lee, Thomas Harrison, John McMillian, Philip Dawe & Gerard Alexander.

Novr. 11th Dr. the Contingent Fund in Acct. with

Paid for Pork to Benja. George 31:18: 6 in Dollars & Cents	106.42
Paid Thomas A. Smith for 22 Barls. & 1 Bushl. Corn 16:13: 0	55.50
Paid Williams for Carter 1:10: 0	5.00
Paid John Matthews Overlooker 15: 0: 0	50.00
Paid Do. for his Wifes Services 6: 6: 0	21.00
Paid Smith 1: 4: 0 & Cooke 1:10: 0	9.00
Paid David Boyle p. Acct. 18: 1:10	60.32
Paid Thomas Davis for Beef 3:14: 8	12.45
Paid Bernard Gallegher 3: 0: 0	10.00
Paid Reids a/c 1:14: 6	5.75
Paid Henry D. Hooe 6: 0: 0	20.00
Paid Bruce for Peyton 1: 2: 0	3.66
Paid John Matthews Balce. a/c 5: 0: 0	16.66
[204] Paid Mr. Dawe 1:10: 0	5.00
Paid Attendance Overseers of the Poor	3.00
Paid Wagonage 3 Loads Corn at 18/ 2:14: 0	9.00
Paid Mr. Muschett for Stocking 18/	3.00
Paid William for 8 pr. of Shoes 2: 8: 0	8.00
Paid for 1000 lb. of Hay at 5/ p.ct. 2:10: 0	8.3-
Paid Sheriffs commission 11:14: 0	39.--
Paid Delinquinces 15: 2: 0	50.3-
	501.--
Amount p. Contra	650.0-
Balance due the County from the Treasurer	148.6-
	650.0-

1801 March 9th to Sale of 395 Acres of Land according to Deed Sold for 16/1 p. Acre	317:12:11
To 3000 lbs. of Tobacco Rent of Sd. Land by bond Sold for 25/ p. hundred	37:10: 0
	355: 2:11
1800 By Cash for Postage & Print'g Advertisemt. for Sale of Land 7/6	7: 6
1801 Do. for the Second Notice 7/6; Do. for 3d Do. 7/6	15: 0
By Cash pd. the Cryer 6/. Do. pd. J. Peyton for Deed 28/	1:14: 0
By Do. pd. John Williams for Copy of Courses	-2:--
	3:--:--
By Commission on ₤ 355: 2:11 at 10 p. Ct.	35:10:--
	38:16: 6
	316: 6: 5
Interest due on the Bonds	14: 1:10
	₤ 330: 8: 3
By Cash pd. John William Gapsep by W. Alexander	₤ 12:--
By Cash pd. H. Dade Hooe for Drawing the Mortgage by William Alexander	₤ 1: 4: 0

1791 By pd. John White for Thomas Wearings two Poor
    Children   15: 0
Dec. 17th By Cash paid Mr. John Grant in part of
    four Poor Children as p. Acct.   1:15:00
                                       William Alexander 4: 6:00
[205] 1790 Samuel Jones's Donation Settled with Mr.
    Cuthbert Bullett for to Cash paid William Alexander   ⅃ 20: 6: 0
Brought up   ⅃ 330: 8: 3

18th November 1802. This Account was Settled by the Commissioners with
the Overseers of the Poor and the above Sum of three hundred & thirty
pounds eight Shillings & three pence paid them as p. Receipt given Sd.
Commissioners & the further Sum of Twenty eight Shillings is to be added
by Capt. McMillian to Sd. Sum.
    Thomas Lee, Thomas Harrison, John McMillian, Philip Dawe, Gerard
Alexander.

INDENTURES, 1749-1782

INDENTURES

(Summarized, With Selected Texts in Full)

Marolen Hawley, bound for the time and term of 21 years to William
Coppage of Hamilton Parish, Fauquirer County. To be taught the trade
of a cordwinder, and to be given (undecipherable) years schooling.
Witnesses: Thomas Whitledge and William Bennitt, February 25, 1764,
(page unnumbered).

*This Indenture made the 25 Day of Febr. in the year of our Lord God
1764 Between Lewis Reno & Howson Hooe Churchwardens of the Parish of
Dettingen in prince william of the one part and William Coppage
Hambelton Parish and of the County of Fauquire of the second Part
Witnesseth That the Said Lewis Reno & Howson Hooe Churchwardens and
order of Court to them Derected Bareing Date the 3 Day of December ...
Hath and by these presents Bind Marolen Hawley an apprentice and
Sarvant unto The Said william Coppage and his Heirs Shall Employ his
Said Sarvant in ... the Said Time and Term of Twenty one years and
the said william Coppage for himself His heirs in consideration
thereof Doth hereby Covenant promiss and agree with Said Lewis Reno
& Howson Hooe Churchwardens that the Said william Coppage Shall and
will Learn him the Said Sarvant the trade of a Cordwinder to Give
him ... Years Schooling also provide for him and alow his Said
Sarvant all necessary Cloths Meat Drink washing and Loding and
all other necessaryes fit and Convenient for the Said Sarvant according
to the Costom of the Contrey and as other Sarvants in Such Cases are
Usually provided for and allowed & In witness whereof the Said
parties have to these present Indenture Interchangeably Set there
hand and Seal the Day and Year firs above written.*

Signed Sealed and Delivered
In the presents off

Thomas Whitledge   *Lewis Reno*

William Bennitt   *Howson Hooe*

                                                William Coppage

John Murphey, a poor baseborn boy, age 2 on June 3 last, bound
until age 21 to Cuthbert Harrison.
Witnesses: none, November 174(undecipherable), (pages 1-2).

This Indenture made the 21st Day of Nover. 174- Between Collo. Benjaman
Grason & Mr. Anthony Seal Church Wardens of the Parish of Dettingen
in the County of prince Wm of the one Part & Cuthbert Harrison of the
afd. Parrish & County of the other Part Witnesseth that the said
Church wardens by Vertue of an order of Vestrey bareing Date the
ninth Day of October 1747 hath Pleased & Bound as an Apprentice Unto
the said Cuthbert Harrison his Heirs & assigns a pore base born boy
named John Murphey aged two years the third Day of June Last after
the Manner of an Apprentice With him the said Harrison to Dwell
untill he shall arive to the age of twenty one years & that the said
Boy Shall not Absent himself out of his said Marsters Service Day
or Night During the term but Shall at all times dureing the terme
aforesaid his said Marsters his heirs & Assigns Well & Truely to be
made serve & Obay in all Such Lawfull Service & Imployments as his
said Master his hears or Assigns shall think Fitt and Requeset &
Shall also Dureing the said term in all things behave himself
Justly & honestly as one in his Station Ought to doe and the said
Cuthbert Harrison for himself his Heirs & Assigns Doth hereby
Convenant to find & Provide unto the said Boy Dureing the term afd.
Sufficiant Clothing & Other Necesseryes that Shall be fitting one in
his Degree and at the Expiration of the Said Term to Pay & allow unto
the Said boy such Corn & Cloths as the Custome Is in the Like Case In
Witness whereof the sd. Church wardens hath Hereunto set there Hands &
Seales & Caused the said Indenture to be Entered on the Regeters of
the sd. Parish the Day & Year above Writen.

Sign Sealed & Delivered
in the Presence of us.

Benja. Grason

Anthony Seal

Joseph Dilon, bound until age 21 to John Simms.   To be taught
to read and write, and the trade and art of a cordwinder.
Witnesses: Thomas Machen and Scarlet Maddon, February 23, 176(undecipherable), (p. 2).

This Indenture made the 23 Day of Febr. in the year of our Lord god
176- Between Howson Hooe & Lewis Reno Churchwardens of the parish of
Dettingin in prince william County of the one part and John Simms of
the Said parish and County of the other part Witnesseth That the
Said Howson Hooe and Lewis Reno Churchwardens by an order of Court to
them Derected Bareing Date the 4 day of Februry. 1765 Hath and by
these Presents Doth Bind Joseph Dilon an apprentice and Sarvant unto
the Said John Simms and to his Heirs and Assigns untell he Shall arrive

to the age of twenty one Years and to Serve the Said John Simms his
Heirs in all Lawfull Employment as the Said John Simms Shall Employ
his Said Sarvant in During the Sd. term tell he Shall arrive to
the age of twenty one years and the Said John Simms and For himself
his Heirs in consideration thereof Doth Covenant Promiss and agree
with the Said Howson Hooe & Lewis Reno Churchwardens that the Said
John Simms Shall and will Learn him The Sd. Joseph Dilon to Read and
wright and Learn him the trade and art of a Cordwinder and also
Provide for an allow his Said Sarvant all necessary Cloaths meat
Drink washing and Lodging And all other necessaryes fit and
Conveniant for him the Said Sarvant According to the Costom of the
Contrey and as other Sarvants in Such cases are Usually provided
for and allowed & In Witness whereof the Said parties have to these
presents Indentures Interchangeably Set there Hands and Seals the
Day and year first above written.

Signed Sealed and Deliverd.
In the present off

Thomas Machen   Howson Hooe

Scarlet Maddon   Lewis Reno

                                           John Simms

Alexander Fullam, a bastard mulatto boy, born March 3, 1748 to
Martha Fullam, bound until age 31 to Richard Blackburn.
Witnesses: Jno. Dawkins and Jno. Cole, January 22, 1750, (p. 3).

Baker Fullam, a bastard mulatto boy, born March 3, 1748 to
Martha Fullam, bound until age 31 to Richard Blackburn.
Witnesses: Jno. Dawkins and Jno. Cole, January 22, 1750, (p. 4).

Giles Burdett, son of John Burdett and Mary his wife deceased,
age 15 on November 10 next, bound until age 21 to John Florance.
To be taught the trade, art and mystery of a tailor, and to read
and write.
Witnesses: Joseph Thurman and John Reno, January 28, 1751, (p. 5).

Mary Pritchet, an orphan girl, born April 9, 1735, bound until
age 18 to Burr Harrison. To be taught to read.
Witnesses: Thos. Young and William Carr, April 9, 1751, (p. 6).

Susannah Pritchet, an orphan girl, born August 24, 1746, bound until age 18 to Burr Harrison. To be taught to read.
Witnesses: Thos. Young and William Carr, April 9, 1751, (p. 7).

Soloman Jones, son of Henry Jones, born June 10, 1749, bound until age 21 to Benjamin Bridges. To be taught to read and write.
Witness: James Muis, April 22, 1751, (p. 8).

Moses Gregg, a bastard child, bound to age 21 to William Carter of Stafford County. To be taught the art, mystery, and trade of house carpenter and joiner, and to write and cipher.
Witnesses: Bertrand Ewell and Benja. Mason, March 24, 1760, (p. 9).

Jonathan Gunn, an orphaned male child, age 15, bound until age 21 to Joseph Davis. To be taught the art and mystery of a cordwinder, and to read and write English.
Witnesses: Simon Luttrell and Thomas Reno, August 21, 1751, (p. 10).

Joseph Parker, born April 30, 1754, bound until age 21 to James Calk. To be taught to read and write, and the trade of a cordwinder and other necessary trades.
Witnesses: William Carr and Bertrand Ewell, March 24, 1760, (p. 11).

Sarah Castilo (also known as Sarah Castilo Elselow), a baseborn or bastard child, born to Ann Castilo on December 2, 1743, bound until age 18 to Scarlet Maddain, planter. To be instructed in Christian principles.
Witnesses: James Tebbs and Nathel. Overall, March 23, 1752, (p. 12).

Eliza. Sias, a girl child, age 4 years on December 1 next, bound until age 18 to Anne Butler, younger.
Witnesses: George Mayson, Philm. Waters, and John Sims, May 25, 1752, (p. 13).

Caleb Blagg, a poor boy, bound until age 21 to James Nisbett. To be taught to read and write, and in the trade of a house carpenter.
Witnesses: Benjamin Grason, Fooshee Tibbs, and Anthony Seale, December 20, 1753, (pp. 14-15).

Samuel Dobbins, orphan, bound for the next 6 years to George
Calvert the younger, shoemaker. To be taught the trade or mystery
of shoemaker.
Witnesses: none, December 20, 1753, (p. 16).

This Indenture Witnesseth that Samuel Dobbins orphan of the County of
Prince William & Parish of Dittingen hath bound himself in the Nature
of an indentured Servent (and by an Order of Court Directed to Richd.
Blackburn & William Tebbs gent. Church Wardens of the Parish afs. &
Dated the 27th Day of Novr. 1753) Unto George Calvert the Younger
Shoemaker to larne his Art trade or Mistry after the Manner of a Servt.
to serve him from the Day of Date hereof, for & Dureing the full tirm
or time of Six Years Next Ensuing all which Time he the said Servent
his Master faithfully Shall Serve his Lawfull Comands Gladly Obay
he shall Do no Damage to his said Master nor Suffer it to be done by
others without letting or giveing Notice thereof to his said Master
he Shall not wast his said Masters goods nor let them Unlawfully to
any, at Cards dice or any unlawfull game he Shall not play whereby
his said Master may be Damaged with his goods or the goods of others
he shall not absent himself Day nor Night from his said Masters
Service without his leave but in all things behave himself as a
faithfull servt. ought to doe Dureing the said time, and the said
Master shall use his best Endeavour to teach or Instruct the sd.
Servt. in the trade or Mistrey he now followeth & provide for him
the said Servt. Sufficient Meat, Drink, Apperel, Washing & Lodging
Dureing the said time, and at the Expiration of the said time, the
said Master to alow him the Custom of the Cuntry as is Usual for
indenterd. servt. as the Law directs. In whereof they have
Interchangeably set there hands & Seales this 20th day of December
1753.

> *Richard Blackrn.*
>
> *William Tibbs*
>
> *George Calvert*

John Kelly, age 1 on September 20, 1753, a baseborn child of
Jane Kelly, servant woman to Mildren Thompson, bound until age 21
to Mildren Thompson, widow. To be given 1 year of schooling, and to
be taught the trade of a house carpenter.
Witness: Susanna Randolph, September 25, 1753, (p. 17).

Sarah Suel, a mulatto girl, age 3 on July 10 next, bound until
age 31 to Richard Jarvis.
Witnesses: Thos. Randolph and Wm. Hughs, January 21, 1754, (p. 18).

William Fewell, an orphan boy, age 10 on March 18 next, bound until age 21 to Benjamin Rush, Junior, blacksmith. To be taught the trade, art or mystery of a blacksmith, and to read and write English. Witnesses: Edward Blackburn, Junr., and Antho. Seale, July 2, 1755, (pp. 19-20).

Moses Jacobs, orphan of William Jacobs, age 7 on May 26, 1756, bound until age 21 to Thos. Homes. To be instructed in the doctrine and tenets of the Church of England, to be given 1 year of schooling, and to find him the trade of a shoemaker. Witnesses: Joseph Thurman and Aaron Fletcher, June 23, 1755, (p. 21).

Elizabeth Rouser, an orphan girl, bound until age 18 to Rachel Spiller. To be taught to read, and to knit, spin, sew, and all other necessary work. Witnesses: William Seale and William Bennett, September 17, 1760, (p. 22).

Pricially Cameron, a baseborn girl child, born January 28, 1754, bound until age 18 to Thos. Hart, Junr. Witnesses: Wm. Durham and Isaac Foster, July 23, 1753, (p. 23).

Phillip Lucas, bastard son, born October 24, 1758 to Hester Lucas, a mulatto, bound until age 31 to Howson Hooe. Witnesses: Thos. Machen and William Tebbs, November 27, 1759, (p. 24).

Virginia Prince Wm. County & Dettingen Parish

To all to whom this Present Indenture shall come We Henry Lee and Lewis Reno Gent. Churchwardens of the parish aforesaid send Greeting Whereas by an Act of Assembly made at the City of Williamsburgh in the year of our Lord One thousand seven hundred and fifty three and in the twenty Seventh year of the Reign of our Sovereign Lord the now King Intituted an Act for the better Government of Servants and Slaves and for other purposes in the said Act mentioned It is therein Enacted that where any female Mullatto or Indian by law Obliged to Serve to the age of thirty one years, hath been or shall be delivered of any Child during the time of Servitude Every Such Child shall Serve the Master or Mistress of Such Mullatto or Indian untill it shall attain the same age the mother of Such Child was by law Obliged to Serve unto,. And Whereas Hester Lucas a Mulatto Woman who was and is obliged by Law to Serve to the age of thirty one years was in the time

of her servitude to Howson Hooe and before She was of the age of
thirty one years delivered of a bastard Child on the twenty fourth
day of October one thousand Seven hundred and Fifty Eight Anno Dom.
named Phillip now Know yee that Wee the said Henry Lee and Lewis
Reno Churchwardens as aforesaid have and do by these presents bind
the Said Bastard Child named Phillip as servant unto Howson Hooe his
heirs or assigns untill he the said Mullatto Bastard Philip Shall
Arrive to and be of the age of thirty one years to Serve and do
any Lawfull work that the said Howson Hooe his heirs or assigns
Shall employ him about for and during the term & time aforesaid, he
or they to find him the Said Philip all things Necessary for one in
his Condition during his Service & the said Howson Hooe doth promise
that at the Expiration of the aforesaid he his &c. Shall & will give
him the Sd. Philip such freedom dues as the Law directs in the Like
cases. In Witness whereof We have hereunto set our hands & Seals
this 27th day of Novr. 1759.

    Signed, Sealed & Delivered
    in Presence of

    Thos. Machen   Henry Lee

    William Tebbs   Lewis Reno

                                           Howson Hooe

    George Cousinbery, son of Mary Cousinbery, bound until age 21
to William Dawkins, blacksmith. To be taught the art, mystery and
occupation of a blacksmith, and to be given 2 years of schooling.
Witnesses: Richard Hardy and Joseph Thurman, May 26, 1755, (pp. 25-26).

This Indenture Made the twenty Sixth day of May in the yeare of our
Lord God one thousand Seven hundred and fifty five Between Mary
Cousinbery and George Cousinbery of the one part and William Dawkins
of Prince William County Blacksmith of the other part Witnesseth
that the said Cousinbery & George Cousinbery by Vertue of the power
and Authority to them Given by An Order of Prince William Court dated
the twenty sixth day of May one thousand Seven Hundred And fifty five,
Do by these presents bind out unto the sd. William Dawkins George
Cousinbery Son of the Aforesaid Mary Cousinbery, untill he the Said
George Shall Attain to twenty one years of Age, and the said William
Dawkins Doth Covenant And Agree to And with the aforesaid Cousinbery
And George Cousinbery to Do his Utmost Endavours to teach or Cause
to be taught and Instructed, his Said Apprentice the Art Mistrey and
Occupation of a blacksmith, the best Way and Manner He can, And to
find for his Said Apprent. during his Service good Wholsom Meate
Washing Lodging And Apparil, And the Said Mary Cousinbery And George
Cousinbery, do Covenant promise And agree with the said William Dawkins
for And in behalf of the Said Apprentice that he the Said Apprentice
Shall behave himself with dilegence and honesty to his Said Master
during his Sd. Apprenticeship, And that he the Sd. Apprenice Shall

not Absent himself from his Masters Service day nor Night Without the
Consent of his Said Master, Ordinaries nor Tipling houses he shall not
Frequent, at Cards or dice he Shall not play, Matrimony he Shall not
Contract During his Apprenticeship Without the Leave of his Said
Master but in all things behave himself as an honest And faithfull
Apprentice towards his Said Master And The Said William Dawkins doth
further Oblige himself to give Unto his Said Apprentice two years
Shooling, at the Expiration of his Servitude, to give him one Suite
of drugget Cloaths. In Witness Whereof Mary Cousenbery And William
Dawkins have to these presents Set there hands and Seales the day
and yeare first Above Written.

Signed, Sealed and Delivered
In the presence of

Richard Hardy

Joseph Thurman

Mary Cousenbury

(her mark)

Wm. Dawkins

Bertrand Ewell

Lewis Reno

George Spiller, bound until age 21 to Rachel Spiller. To be taught to read and write, and the art of weaving. Witnesses: John Reno, Junr., Haden Edwards and William Tackett, February 21, 1761, (p. 26).

Eleanor Childs, an orphan, bound until age 18 to Joseph Butler and Ann his wife. To be taught to sew, knit and spin. Witnesses: Antho. Seale and Thos. Machen, February 18, 1756, (p. 27).

Benjamin Thomas, orphan of William Thomas, deceased, age 11, bound until age 21 to Benjamin Rush. To be taught the art, mystery, and occupation of a cooper, and to read and write. Witnesses: Benjamin Mason, Francis Reno, Francis Jackson and James Gregsby, May 25, 1761, (p. 28).

William Cousenbery, son of Mary Cousenbery, bound until age 21 to Wm. Dawkins. To be taught the art and mystery of a blacksmith. Witness: John Dawkins, May 26, 1755, (pp. 29-30).

Spencer Pearce, an orphan male child, born August 23, 1762, bound until age 21 to John Glasscock or his daughter Margaret Glasscock. To be taught the art and mystery of a weaver, to read and write distinctly, and the Lords Prayer, the Creed and Ten Commandments contained in the Church catechism, and be brought up in a Christianlike manner.
Witnesses: Charles Porter and Nicholas George, Junr., June 20, 1764, (p. 30).

Elisha Denis, a male child, said to be age 4 September 1 next, bound until age 21 to Wm. Lashbrooke. To be taught the shoemaker's trade.
Witnesses: Edward Gwatkin and John Whitledge, May 21, 1756, (p. 31).

John Crupper, a poor child, bound until age 21 to Jacob Colvert. To be taught the trade, science or occupation of a house carpenter.
Witnesses: Burr Harrison and Matt. Harrison, March 14, 1756, (pp. 32-33).

Elizabeth Mason, an orphan, bound until age 18 to Nicholas Brown. To be taught to read, spin, knit, and sew.
Witnesses: John Chesser and James Peake, (no month) 4, 1763, (p. 34).

Collin Dilon, bound until age 21 to Scarlett Madden. To be taught to read and write, and the trade and art of a cordwinder.
Witnesses: John Simms and Thomas Machen, February 23, 1769, (p. 34).

Thomas Grigory, a mulatto bastard child, born September 21 last to Christian Grigory, a white woman, servant to John Hooe, bound to age 31 to John Hooe.
Witness: Benjamin Rush, September 5, 1763, (p. 35).

James, bastard male child, born July 24, 1764 to Hester Lucas, a mulatto woman, servant to Howson Hooe, bound until age 31 to Howson Hooe.
Witnesses: Benjamin Rush and John Peyton, June 4, 1765, (p. 36).

Francis, bastard female child, born July 28, 1761 to Hester Lucas, a mulatto woman, servant to Howsen Hooe, bound until age 31 to Howsen Hooe.
Witnesses: James Ingoe Dozer and Daniel Kincheloe, May 3, 1763, (p. 37).

Gabriel Muffett, son of Gabriel Muffett, deceased, bound until age 21 to Lynaugh Helm. To be taught to read and write, and the trade of a house carpenter.
Witness: James Hathaway, September 5, 1763, (p. 38).

Linna Dennis, an orphan girl, bound until age 18 to Ann Farrow. To be taught to read, spin, knit and sew.
Witnesses: John Baxter and John Chesser, May 8, 1764, (p. 39).

Amos Shadburn, a poor boy three years or thereabouts, bound until age 21 to Leonard Hart. To be taught the trade of shoemaker.
Witness: John Chambers, August 24, 1763, (p. 40).

George Singclear, bound until age 21 to Ruben Ellot. To be taught the trade and art of a cooper.
Witnesses: William Bryce and John Riddle, February 22, 1765, (p. 40).

Waymon Sinclear, bound until age 21 to Ruben Ellot. To be taught to read and write, and the trade and art of a cooper.
Witnesses: William Bryce and John Riddell, February 23, 1765, (p. 41).

John Bell, an orphan, bound until age 21 to Charles Davis. To be taught the trade and art of saddle making.
Witnesses: Thomas Chapman and Francis Reno, (blank), 1765, (p. 41).

Dennis Larey, an orphan child, bound until age 21 to Valentine Clannigal. To be taught to read and write, and the trade and art of a farming business.
Witnesses: William Tackett and James Peak, (blank), 1765, (p. 42).

John Williams, orphan, bound until age 21 to Peter Forman. To be taught the trade and art of wagon maker.
Witnesses: Jenkens Deveaney and Michll. Gretter, March 5, 1765, (p. 42).

Catharine Mitchell, orphan of Jededean Mitchell, deceased, bound until the lawful age to Thomas Buchard. To be taught to read, sew, knit and spin.
Witness: none, March 16, 1763, (p. 43).

James Randolph, orphan, bound until age 21 to Alexander Rigby. To be taught the art, mystery, and trade of a house and shop joiner, and to read and write.
Witnesses: William Dobies and Thomas Machen, May 6, 1763, (p. 43).

Mary Combs, bound until age 18 to Thomas Attwell. To be taught to read, spin, sew and knit.
Witnesses: Foushee Tebbs and Danl. Peyne, October 10, 1765, (p. 44).

John Dearen, an orphan male child, bound until age 21 to Nicholas George, Junr. To be taught to read and write, and the Lords Prayer, Creed and Ten Commandments containing the church catechism, and be brought up in a Christianlike manner, and the art and mystery of a shoemaker.
Witnesses: Bertrand Ewell and John Gunyon, June 4, 1764, (p. 44).

Presley Grigory, a mulatto bastard, born about 12 months ago to Christian Grigory, a Christian white woman, servant to John Hooe, bound until age 31 to John Hooe.
Witnesses: Francis Stripling and John Smith, September 3, 1764, (p. 45).

Mary Forbess (Forbuss), a mulatto bastard, about 3 years old, born to Isbal Forbess, a Christian white woman, servant to Jemima Hewett, bound until age 31 to Jemima Hewett.
Witnesses: John Hooe and John Reeve, August 25, 1764, (p. 46).

James Forbess, a mulatto bastard about 18 months of age, born to
Isbal Forbess, a Christian white woman, servant to Moses Reeve, bound
until age 31 to Moses Reeve (Reaves).
Witnesses: John Hooe and John Reeve, August 25, 1764, (p. 47).

Thomas Machen, an orphan, bound until age 21 to Thomas Johnson
Price, bricklayer. To be taught to read and write, and the trade of
a bricklayer.
Witnesses: Lynaugh Helm and Hubberd Prince, May 5, 1767, (p. 48).

Bazel Hollis, a poor boy, bound until age 21 to Leonard Hart.
Witness: Jeremiah Moore, November 7, 1767, (p. 49).

William Robertson (Robison), son of Sarah Robertson, bound until
age 21 to Benjamin Johnson. To be taught to read and write, and the
trade of a shoemaker.
Witnesses: Thomas Blackburn and William Carr, September 8, 1767,
(p. 50).

Robert Stanhope, an orphan, 9 years of age next September, bound
until age 21 to William Martin (Martain). To be taught the business
of a shoemaker, and given 1 year of schooling.
Witness: none, February 19, 1767, (p. 51).

Jane Overall, daughter of Thomas Overall, bound until age 18 to
William Anness. To be taught to read, and the trade of a weaver.
Witnesses: Timothy Peyton and John Roye, February 1, 1768, (p. 52).

Zechariah Reed, an orphan of John Reed, deceased, bound until age
21 to John Holliday. To be taught to read and write, and the trade of
a shoemaker.
Witnesses: John Simms and Timothy Peyton, February 1, 1768, (p. 53).

John Robertson, a poor boy, bound until age 21 to John Leatherwood,
cordwainer. To be taught to read and write, and the trade of a shoemaker.
Witnesses: William Grayson and Rob. Harrison, September 7, 1767,
(p. 54).

Moses Grigg, a baseborn male child, bound until age 21 to James Carter Butler, joiner. To be taught the trade of a house joiner. Witness: Jo. Williams and Richard Rixey, Junr., September 5, 1768, (p. 55).

Thomas Cole, baseborn child of Phoebe Cole, a free negro, bound until age 21 to William Bennett, inspector. To be taught the trade and art of a carpenter.
Witnesses: Thomas Reno, Juner., George Carter, and Moses Moss, June 10, 1768, (p. 56).

Robert Cole, a baseborn child of Phoebe Cole, a free negro, bound until age 21 to William Bennett, inspector. To be taught the trade and art of shoemaking.
Witnesses: Thomas Reno, Juner., George Carter, and Moses Moss, June 10, 1768, (p. 57).

Joseph Cole, baseborn child of Phoebe Cole, a free negro, bound until age 21 to William Bennett, inspector. To be taught the trade and art of a house carpenter.
Witnesses: John Britt, Daniel Kincheloe, and James Muschet, September 7, 1768, (p. 58).

Catharine Cole, baseborn daughter of Phoebe Cole, a free negro, bound until the age according to law to William Bennett.
Witnesses: John Britt, Daniel Kincheloe and James Muschet, September 7, 1768, (p. 59).

Winifred Minor Umpriss Harper, bound until age 18 to Jacob Holtsclaw. To be taught to read, sew, knit and spin.
Witnesses: John Buchanan and Wm. Brent, May 11, 1768, (p. 60).

Thomas Milton, an orphan boy, bound until age 21 to Thomas Reeve (Reaves), turner. To be taught the art of turning.
Witness: Henry Dade Hooe, (Blank), 1767, (p. 61).

Jinny Reid, daughter of John Reid, deceased, bound until age 18 to John Holladay. To be taught to sew, spin and knit, and to read. Witnesses: Orig Young and Cornelious Kincheloe, October 2, 1769, (p. 62).

George Adam Gardinhire, orphan of Jacob Gardinhire, age 14, bound until age 21 to William Lindsey. To be taught to read and write, and the trade of a joiner. Witness: none, December 4, 1769, (p. 63).

America Wilfred, male, bound until age 21 to William Reno. To be taught to read and write, and the trade of a shoemaker. Witnesses: Orig Young and Cornelious Kincheloe, October 2, 1769, (p. 64).

Charles Edwards, son of Elisabeth Edwards, 1 year of age on November 27 last, bound until age 21 to Silvester Moss. Witness: Mary Peyton, March 12, 1770, (p. 65).

Valentine White, male orphan, bound until age 21 to Valentine Cloneger. To be taught to read and write, and the trade and art of a farming business. Witnesses: Lewis Reno and Wm. Tebbs, November 7, 1769, (p. 66).

Thomas Sumerset, orphan, bound until age 21 to Valentine Cloninger. To be taught to read and write, and the trade and art of a farming business. Witness: John Murray, July 2, 1770, (p. 67).

Alexander Bell, about 18 years of age January 2 by his own account, bound until age 21 to John Wyatt. To be taught the occupation of a planter. Witnesses: Henry Peyton, Junr., and Willm. Turley, May 18, 1770, (p. 68).

Alexander Edison, age 16 on this March 28, bound until age 21 to Thomas R. Reeve. To be taught the art and mystery of farming. Witnesses: Henry Lee and Henry Peyton, March 5, 1770, (p. 69).

Hannah Boyd, female mulatto bastard, born February 17, 1768 to Elisabeth Boyd, formerly a servant to Charles Chaddock, bound until age 18 to Charles Chaddock. To be brought up in a Christianlike manner.
Witnesses: Wm. Alexander and Henry Peyton, August 2, 1773, (p. 70).

James Mathias Bryan, orphan of John Bryan, born July 20, 1765, bound until age 21 to Richard Mathias Switman. To be taught to read and write, and the trade of a tailor.
Witnesses: James Price Posey and James Conduct, July 3, 1773, (p. 71).

John Hulitt, orphan, bound until age 21 to Thomas Stone. To be taught the ordinary trade of shoemaking.
Witnesses: Geo. Bigby and Nimrod Hamrick, January 9, 1773, (p. 71).

John Bryan, orphan, age 5 next May, bound to age 21 to William Slade. To be taught the trade of a shoemaker, and given 1 year of schooling.
Witnesses: Henry D. Hooe and Joseph Blackwell, November 25, 1773, (p. 73).

Thomas Splawn, a poor boy, bound until age 21 to John Jones, joiner. To be taught the trade of a joiner.
Witnesses: William Alexander and Henry D. Hooe, September 7, 1773, (p. 74).

William McFee, orphan of John and Susannah McFee, born May 3, 1770, bound to Zephaniah Crook, planter. To be taught the art and mystery of a shoemaker, and to write and read English distinctly, and the Lords Prayer, the Creed and Ten Commandements contained in the Church catechism and be brought up in a Christianlike manner.
Witnesses: Benjamin Hamrick and Benjamin Fewel, April 7, 1775, (p. 75).

John Rose, age 11, bound until age 21 to William Jenkins of the
Town of Dumfries. To be taught to read and write, and the trade of
a barber.
Witnesses: Boyd Reid and Thos. Davis, February 4, 1777, (p. 76).

Rhrora McKinsie, son of Murdock McKensie (the said Rhrora
McKensie being born at sea), age 4 years and 2 months, bound until
age 21 to John Murray. To be taught to read and write.
Witness: Evan Williams, July 7, 1777, (p. 77).

Milly Thomas, a mulatto bastard girl, age 2½, bound until age
21 to Fanny Melton.
Witness: Evan Williams, September 2, 1777, (p. 78).

Michael Lenox, male orphan of Lawrence Lenox, age 5, bound until
age 21 to Michael Ferrell (Ferrel, Farrell, Farrel). To be given
schooling, and to be taught the trade of a shoemaker.
Witness: Wm. Whitledge, May 20, 1775, (p. 79).

Sarah Lenox, orphan of Lawrence Lenox, age 12, bound until age 18
to Michael Farrell, (Farrel). To be given schooling.
Witness: Wm. Whitledge, March 17, 1775, (p. 80).

David Cooper, age 9 December 28 next, child of John Cooper,
deceased, who left to his wife, Susan Cooper, to put his son to
a trade, bound until age 21 to Carty Wells, Senr., of Stafford
County. To be taught the trade and business of a farmer, and given
18 months schooling.
Witness: Nicholas George, November 10, 1777, (p. 81).

Ann Wyatt, a mulatto bastard girl, age (blank), bound until age
18 to John McMillian, Gent. To be taught to read and write, and
some suitable trade or employment.
Witness: Evan Williams, February 9, 1779, (p. 82).

James Baptist Mattingly, male about 11 years of age, bound until age 21 to Travers Nash of Fauquier County. To be taught to read and write, and the trade of a shoemaker.
Witnesses: Evan Williams and Robt. H. Hooe, October 24, 1778, (p. 83).

Sarah Jones, age 9, orphan of Frans. Jones, bound until age 18 to William Roundtree. To be taught to read and write, and to be taught some suitable employment.
Witness: Evan Williams, June 8, 1779, (p. 84).

John Jones, an orphan child, age 12½, bound until age 21 to Anne Vaughan. To be taught to read and write, and the trade of a weaver.
Witness: Evan Williams, April 7, 1799, (p. 85).

Margaret Mattocks, a baseborn child, 6 years of age, bound until age 18 to Colin Campbell. To be taught to read and write, and to be taught some suitable trade or employment.
Witness: Evan Williams, May 3, 1780, (pp. 86-87).

Elizabeth Scurlock, a poor child of about 9 years of age, bound until age 18 to Simon Davis. To be taught to read and write, and taught some useful trade or employment.
Witness: Evan Williams, November 3, 1779, (pp. 87-88).

Simon Thomas, orphan of John Thomas, age (blank), bound until age 21 to Joseph Stephens. To be taught to read and write, and the trade of (blank).
Witness: Evan Williams, August 8, 1780, (pp. 88-89).

Rhody Fanning, a poor boy, 7 years of age, bound until age 21 to James Roach. To be taught to read and write, and the trade of (blank).
Witness: Evan Williams, September 5, 1780, (pp. 89-90).

Simpson Hutchinson, orphan of John Hutchinson, age 14, bound until age 21 to Philip Dawe. To be taught to read and write, and the trade of a silversmith.
Witness: Evan Williams, November 10, 1780, (pp. 91-92).

William Gunyon, orphan of John Gunyon, age 14, bound until age 21 to John Murray. To be taught to read and write.
Witness: Evan Williams, April 4, 1781, (pp. 92-93).

Wm. McDaniel, 10 years of age, a baseborn child of Mima King, bound until age 21 to Timothy King. To be taught to read and write, and the trade of a shoemaker.
Witness: Evan Williams, November 7, 1781, (pp. 93-94).

Nancy Binks, an orphan child, 5 years of age, bound until age 18 to James Barber. To be taught to read and write, and taught some suitable trade or employment.
Witness: Evan Williams, February 5, 1782, (pp. 94-95).

Rhuben Herndon, a baseborn boy about 18 months of age, bound until age 21 to Soloman Jones, Gent. To be taught to read and write, and the trade of a shoemaker.
Witness: Evan Williams, September 4, 1782, (pp. 95-96).

This indenture made the fourth day of September one thousand seven hundred and Eighty two Between James Nisbitt and Jesse Ewell Gentlemen Church Wardens of the parish of Dettingen in the County of Prince William of the one part and Soloman Jones of the said Parish and County Gent. of the other part Witnesseth that in pursuance of an order of the Worshipfull the Court of Prince William bearing Date the 2d day of Septr. 1782. directed to them the said James Nisbett and Jesse Ewell they the said James Nisbett and Jesse Ewell as Churchwardens as afd. Do bind unto the said Soloman Jones Rhuben Herndon a base Born Child untill he the said Rhuben shall attain the age of twenty one years being at the time about Eighteen Months old to serve the said Soloman Jones in all lawful Employments until he the said Rhuben Shall attain the age of twenty one years as aforesaid And the said Soloman Jones for himself doth hereby promise and agree to & with the said James Nisbett and Jesse Ewell & their Successors that the said Soloman Jones Shall and will Cause the said Rhuben Herndon to be taught to read and write and also Learn

him the trade of a Shoemaker and further Shall and will for and During
the term afd. find and provide the sd. Rhuben with good and Sufficeint
meat Drink washing Lodging and apparell according to the custom of
the Country and on his Coming of age pay him the same freedom Dues
as by law allowed for imported indented Servants. In Consideration
whereof the said Rhuben Herndon is well and truly to serve the said
Soloman Jones the term afd. his Secrets keep and all Lawfull commands
obey. In Witness Whereof the said parties to these presents have
hereunto Set their hands and Seals the Day and year first Within
Written.

     Sealed and Delivered
     in presence of

     Evan Williams   James Nisbett

                                                     Jesse Ewell

                                                     Soloman Jones

                                                     (his mark)

APPENDIX

APPENDIX

The following entries appear on the pages immediately preceding the minutes of the Vestry.

The oath appears to carry the actual signatures of the subscribers, as distinguished from the names appearing after the notation <u>Signed</u> in the minutes of the Vestry and of the Overseers of the Poor, which seem uniformly to be in the hand of the clerks.

(Illegible) *Register of Overwharton Parish.*

I do so declare that I do believe (illegible) *Sacrament of the Lords Suppor or in the Elements of bread* (illegible) *after the Consecration thereof by any person whatsoever.*

July 25th 1748	*John Whitledge*
Augt. 23d, 1748	*Foushe Tebbs*
Sepr. 26th, 1748	*Bertrand Ewell*
(Illegible) 27, 1748	*Willm. Roussau, Jno. Crump*
29th Novr. 1748	*Lewis Reno*
28 March 1749	*John Frogg*
22d May 1749	*Thos. Harrison, Jos.*(undecipherable)*, R. Blackburn, Val. Peyton, John Wright, Antho. Seale, Benja. Bullett, Robt. Wickliff, Jno. Bell*
24th May 1749	*John Frogg*
25th May 1749	*John Copedge*
26th June 1749	*John Wright, R. Blackburn, Val. Peyton, Antho. Seale, Howson Kenner, R. Wickliff*
24th July 1749	*Bertrand Ewell, Timo. Thornton*
20th Augt. 1749	*Wm. Ellzey*
25th Sept. 1749	*John Frogg, Jno.*(undecipherable)*, William Eustace, Val. Peyton, Th. Peyton, John Crump, John Copedge*
26 Sept. 1749	*Benja. Bullett, Wm.*(undecipherable)*, Jno. Crump,* (undecipherable)*, Bertrand Ewell,*

<pre>
                          Robt. Wickliff, Pet. Wagener

27 November 1749   Thos. Harrison, R. Blackburn, Jos. Hudnell,
                         Antho. Seale, Howson Kenner, Jas. Nisbett,
                         J. Ball, Cuthbt. Harrison, John Copedge,
                         Richd. Kenner, Bertrand Ewell, (illegible)

28th Nov. 1749   (illegible), Benja. Bullitt, William Tebbs
</pre>

Also preceding the minutes of the Vestry is the following entry:

*Taken from the Register of Overwharton Parish. Burr Harrison now
or Late of Chappawamsic In this Parish and County Son to Cuthbert
Harrison was babtised in the parish of Sant Margretts, Westminster
the 28th day of december 1637 As by Certificate ... under the hand of
Thomas Wiver Registerer for the sd. parish to me did appeare.*

                                        Richard Gibson

*Thomas the son of the said Burr Harrison was born September the
7th day 1665. And departed this life on the 13th day of August at 2
in the Morning 1746 Burr Harrison the son of the said Thos. Harrison
was born May the 21st 1699.*
   *Thomas the son of the said Burr Harrison was born March the 3rd
1723.*
   1. *Jane the daughter of the said Burr Harison was born the 9th
      day of December 1726.*
   2. *Seth the daughter of the said Burr Harrison was born the 30th
      day of November 1729.*

On the unnumbered page preceding page 1 of the Indentures appears
the following entry:

*Benja. the Son of Thomas and Ann Harrison was borne a Saturday at
Six a Clock in the moring the 17th day of August 1744. Ann the
Daughter of Thomas and Ann Harrison was Born a Sunday the 29th day of
October 1749.*

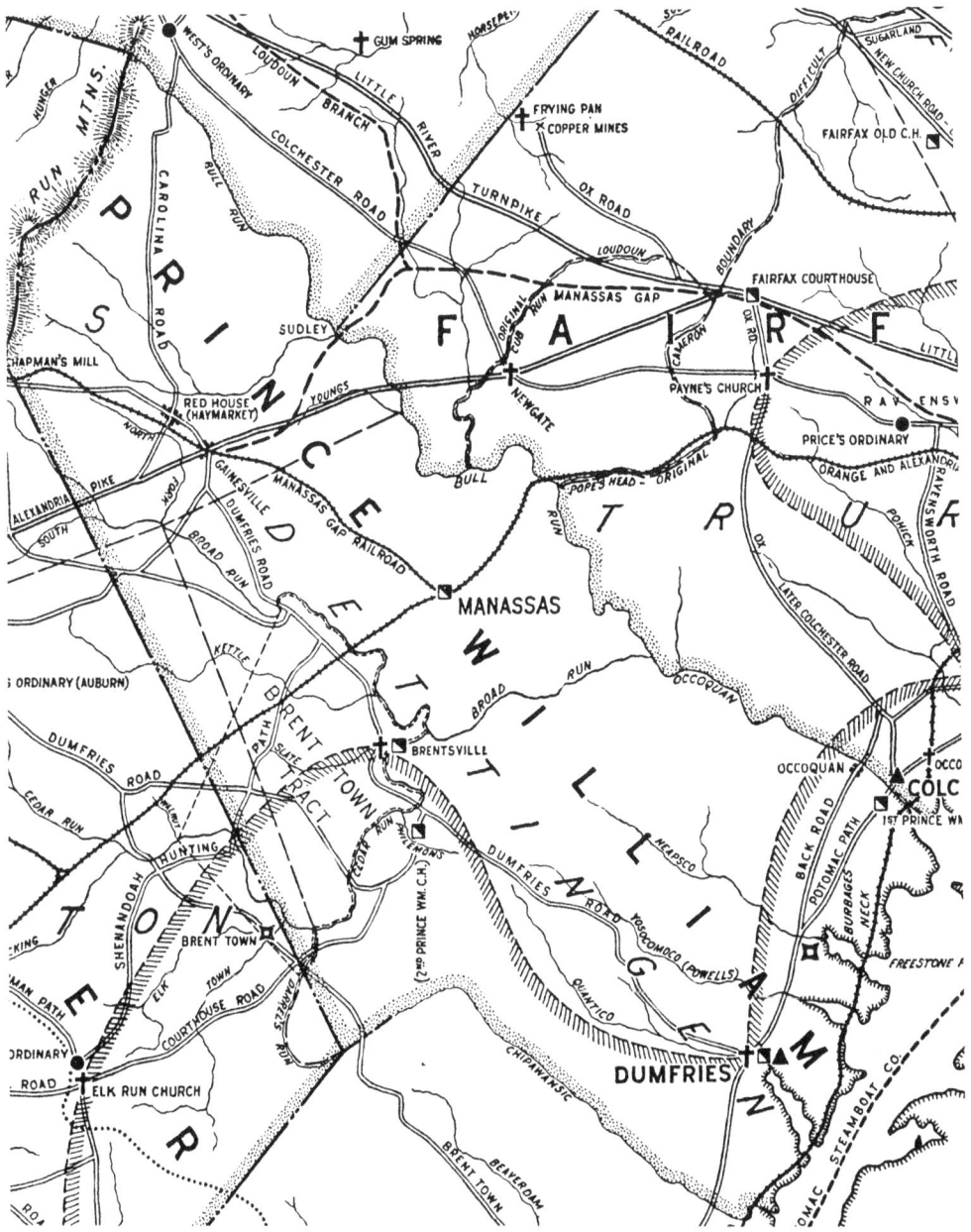

From FAIRFAX HARRISON, *Landmarks of Old Prince William*, by permission of the Virginia Book Company, Berryville, Virginia.

INDEX

INDEX OF SURNAMES

Bigby (Bigbey), 34, 36, 48, 50
  118

Binks, 74, 121

Bird, 27, 40, 70-71

Blackburn, 1-2, 4-5, 7, 9-13,
  15-21, 51-52, 55-62, 64-66,
  106, 108-109, 115, 123-124

Blackwell, 118

Blagg, 107

Blair, 33

Blancett, 91

Bland, 3, 8-9, 11, 17, 20, 28,
  33, 38, 42, 48

Bobos, 81-82

Boggess, 29, 32

Bogle, 3

Bonam, 42

Bosswel, 50

Bowers, 57

Bowin, 24

Bowling, 33

Boyd, 118

Boyle, 102

Brady, 86

Brawner, 83

Brent, 45, 47, 49, 63, 116

Brett, 32

Brewer, 86

Bridges, 107

Briscoe, 6, 9

Bristo (Brister, Bristor,
  Bristow), 6, 8-14, 16-17, 19,
  69, 71, 73, 76

Britt, 10, 18, 23, 30, 40, 116

Bronaugh, 95

Brown, 40, 43, 56, 72, 74-75,
  97, 112

Bruce, 85-94, 98-99, 102

Brundige, 87

Bryant (Bryan, Bryn.), 1, 3-6,
  8, 10, 30, 32-33, 35, 47, 71,
  73, 75, 77, 81, 118

Bryce, 113

Buchanan, 24-29, 31-34, 36-37,
  39-42, 44-45, 116

Buchard, 114

Bullitt (Bullett), 34, 45-48,
  51-53, 55-62, 64-65, 68, 72,
  74, 93, 97, 103, 123-124

Bunn, 69, 81

Burdett, 106

Burroughs, 95

Butler, 1-7, 9, 14, 21, 23,
  95, 107, 111, 116

Calk, 3, 6-7, 21, 30, 107

Calvert, 27, 30, 33, 35-39, 43,
  48, 50, 54, 61, 74, 85-86, 108

Cameron, 109

Campbell, 69-70, 120

Cane, 50

Canterbury, 5

Carey, 89

Carpenter, 22, 24, 47-48

Carr, 4, 6, 8-14, 16-29, 31-43,
  45-67, 69-70, 72-73, 76,
  87-88, 106-107, 115

Carter, 27-36, 38-39, 41-42,
  52, 54, 78-79, 102, 107, 116

Casey, 69, 71, 73, 75, 77, 80

Caster (Castor), 32, 37-38

Castilo, 107

Catlett, 39

Chaddock, 118

Chambers, 113

Chamblin, 35

Champ, 6

Champney, 3

Chapman, 36, 39, 43, 45-46,
  48-50, 52, 54, 59, 63, 65,
  78, 81, 84, 88, 100, 113

Cheek, 62, 65-66, 73

Cheshire (Chesher, Chesser,
  Chesshire), 37-38, 48, 50,
  52-53, 55-58, 60-61, 63-64, 66,
  72, 76, 78, 112-113

Chester, 8

Childs, 111

Chinn, 45, 52

Clannigal, 113

Clerk, 23

Cleveland, 41

Cloneger (Cloninger), 117

Coffer, 35

Colberts, 12

Cole (Coles), 6, 76, 78, 88-89,
  91, 106, 116

Collen, 47

Colvert, 112

Combs, 114

Conduct, 118

Congrove, 8

Conner, 17

Cooke, 3, 98, 102

Coon, 65

Cooper, 28, 57, 59-60, 76, 119

Copia, 17

Coppage (Copage, Copege), 37-38,
59, 104, 123-124

Coram (Corin, Corrin, Corum), 6,
34-36, 38, 41, 43-44, 46,
48-49, 52

Corben, 50

Cornhil, 69, 71, 73, 75, 77, 80

Cornish, 36

Cornwell (Cornwil, Cornwill),
29, 31-33, 35-36, 38-41,
43-44, 46, 48-49, 52-55, 61,
86, 90

Cotril, 74

Cotter, 29, 42

Cousinbery (Cousenbery), 79
81, 110-111

Cowell, 21

Cox, 57

Cristia, 69

Crook, 42-43, 58-61, 63-64,
66, 118

Croson, 69, 71, 73, 75, 77, 80

Crouch, 24, 33, 35

Crump, 16, 123

Crupper, 112

Curry, 54-55

Curtess, 45

D

Dade, 81

Dalgam (Delgarn, Dilgarn), 13-14,
16, 48

Dallis, 56

Dalton, 29, 31, 33-34, 36, 38-39,
45

Danil, 81

Davis (Davice), 9-10, 21, 40, 54,
63, 74, 78, 86, 102, 107, 113,
119-120

Dawe, 65, 77-96, 98-100, 102-103

Dawkins, 106, 110-111

Dawson, 2

Dean, 42-44, 49-50

Dearen, 114

Delany, 57, 61, 63, 65

Demsdell, 46

Dennis (Denis), 112-113

Deskin (Deskins, Diskin, Diskins),
1-2, 4-5, 7, 10-13, 15-23, 33

Deveaney, 114

Dial, 61

Dilon, 105-106, 112

Dobbins, 108

Dobies, 114

Doubty (Doughty), 69, 71, 73, 75-77, 80, 89

Doudal, 82

Douglas, 22, 24, 28, 101

Douncon, 17

Dounman, 59

Dounton, 83, 86

Dowell, 23, 72

Doyle, 79

Dozer, 113

Driskel, 52

Drue, 54

Drummond, 28

Drury, 69

Dunavin, 74, 76

Dunlop, 38

Durham, 109

Durmon, 69

Dye, 74

<u>E</u>

Eady, 22

Ealse, 66

Earle (Earls), 61, 63-64, 66, 69, 71-73, 75, 77, 80

Eaves, 55

Eavins, 37

Edie, 31

Edison, 118

Edoo, 36

Edwards, 40, 43, 111, 117

Ellis, 74, 78, 80-81

Ellot, 113

Ellzey (Elizey, Elzey), 32-33, 35-37, 39-40, 44-51, 53, 123

Emmanuel, 59

Ennis, 71

Espay, 78

Estep, 16

Eustace, 123

Evans, 99

Ewell, 1-5, 9, 11-23, 53-68, 70-78, 107, 111, 114, 121-124

<u>F</u>

Fanning, 120

Fare (Faire), 69, 71, 73, 75 77, 80

Farrow, 3, 19, 24, 33, 37, 40, 113

Fegan (Feagins, Fegans), 3-4, 48

Ferguson (Farguson, Fergason, Forguson), 1-7, 9, 11-12, 15, 40, 83

Ferrell (Farrel, Farrell, Ferrel), 119

Fewel (Fewell), 109, 118

Finch, 63

Fitzhugh, 62-67, 69-70

Fletcher, 109

Florance, 4

Floyd, 27-28, 35

Foley (Folley), 8, 35

Fonworthy, 64

Forbus (Forbes, Forbess, Forbis,
   Forbuss), 39, 53, 57, 59, 61,
   66, 69-71, 73, 75, 77, 80,
   84, 89, 101, 114-115

Ford, 30, 79, 81, 83

Forgey (Forgy), 54, 56

Forman, 114

Forscythe (Forseythe, Forsithe),
   70, 74, 76, 83

Foster (Fooster), 18-19, 23,
   39, 109

Foulkner, 39

Fox, 84

Foxworthy (Foxworth), 70-71,
   74-75, 77, 80, 91, 95, 99-101

Frogg, 123

Fullam (Fullum), 5, 72, 78, 106

G

Gallahue, 30

Gallegher (Galligher), 78, 81,
   98, 102

Ganett, 71

Gapsep, 102

Gardinhire, 117

Garrison, 71

George, 71, 102, 112, 114, 119

German (Germin), 47, 50

Gibson, 21, 31, 33, 45, 50, 83,
   124

Giles, 24

Glasscock, 112

Godwood, 71, 74-75, 77-78, 82

Gooch, 2

Gradey, 35

Graham (Grayham), 4, 17, 19-20,
   22-24, 26, 28-29, 31, 33-34,
   36, 38-39, 42-44, 46, 50, 54,
   56-57, 59-61, 63-64, 66, 72,
   78, 83

Grant, 1, 103

Gray (Grey), 48-49

Grayson (Grason), 1-13, 15,
   17-18, 20-23, 35, 65, 67-68,
   105, 107, 115

Green, 45, 50

Gregg, 2, 7, 10, 107

Greggrey, 10

Gregsby, 111

Greniore, 78

Gretter, 114

Griffin, 27

Grigg, 116

Grigory, 112, 114

Grinstead (Grenstead), 30, 38, 45, 70-73, 75-77, 79, 81, 83, 86

Gunn, 32-33, 35, 37-39, 41 43, 107

Gunyan (Gunyon), 45, 114, 121

Guy, 82

Gwatkin (Gwatkins), 67-68, 70-73, 75-76, 112

Gwinn (Gwin), 24, 27, 35, 50

H

Haley, 21

Hall, 24

Halladay, 39

Hamilton (Hamelton, Hamlinton), 33, 35-36, 38, 65-66, 69, 71, 73, 75, 77, 80, 83

Hammel, 95

Hamrick, 21, 69, 71, 73, 78, 80, 118

Hancock, 40

Hannon, 42, 45-46

Hardin, 52, 82

Harding, 22-23

Hardy, 110-111

Harper, 116

Harris, 24, 48, 79, 81

Harrison, 1, 3-4, 6-11, 13-27, 29-31, 33-34, 36-37, 39, 41-45, 48-51, 53, 59, 77-103, 105-107, 112, 115, 123-124

Hart, 47, 109, 113, 115

Harvey, 54, 56

Hathaway, 113

Hawley, 104

Hay, 92

Haywood, 55, 57, 59

Hazelrigg (Hazelridge, Hazelrig), 21-22, 24, 63

Hedges, 8, 21, 24, 70-71, 73, 75, 77-78, 81

Hees, 65

Helm, 39-49, 51-58, 62, 65-66, 77-84, 86, 88, 93-95, 97, 113, 115

Henderson, 28-29, 33, 35, 83

Herndon, 121-122

Hewett, 114

Hickerson, 58

Hides, 29

Higgs, 34, 38

Highwarden, 74

Hogan, 3-4, 6

Holladay (Holliday), 24, 117

Hollis, 115

Holtsclaw, 116

Homes, 109

Hooe, 24-29, 31-34, 36-42,
44-45, 47-59, 61-62, 64-80,
82-94, 97-98, 101-102,
104-106, 110, 112-116, 118,
120

Horman, 3, 5-6

Horsenail, 81

Horton, 60, 63, 65, 70

Hudnell, 124

Hughs, 108

Hulitt, 118

Humes, 55

Hunter, 78, 82-83

Hurley, 72, 74

Hutchinson, 120-121

J

Jackson, 10, 21, 111

Jacobs, 109

Jameson, 83, 95

Jarvice, 18, 108

Jeffries (Jeffres), 31, 33
35-36, 38-39, 41, 43-44, 46,
50, 52, 54-55, 58-61, 63-64,
66, 70-72, 74, 76-78, 80, 83

Jenkins, 119

Johnson, 28, 30-31, 33, 35-36,
38, 41-46, 48-49, 52-53, 55-61,
98, 115

Johnston, 19, 31-32, 38, 62, 64,
66

Jones, 9, 11, 24, 27-28, 50, 54,
72, 88, 91, 93-94, 97, 99, 101,
103, 107, 118, 120-122

Junkinson, 4, 8

Justise, 3-4, 6, 8-9

K

Keith, 3, 49

Kelly, 46, 54, 108

Kendall (Kendal, Kindal), 47-49,
52

Kenner (Kinner), 16, 123-124

Kent, 24, 27-28, 30

Keys, 89

Killy, 74

Kincheloe, 41, 67-68, 70, 72-73,
75-76, 113, 116-117

McAvoy (McAboy, Maccavoy), 50
  55, 76

McDaniel (McDaniels, McDanil),
  22, 64, 83, 121

McDonald, 24

McDonough (McDonaugh), 40, 52

McFee, 46-47, 118

McGuire, 7

McIntosh, 72, 74, 76, 78

McKensie, 70-71, 119

McMahon, 75, 77, 80

McMillion, 27, 29, 32, 63-67, 70
  85-103, 119

Melton, 119

Meroney (Merroney, Monrony),
  18, 20-21, 23-26

Metcalf, 28, 32

Miles, 21-22, 24

Millinder, 59

Milner (Milliner), 63, 65-66,
  89

Milstead, 46

Milton, 116

Mitchell (Michell), 31, 35, 63,
  95, 114

Mitchem, 16-17, 19-20, 22

Mollahon, 30

Monroe, 46

Montgomerie, 50

Mooney, 58-59, 61

Moore (More), 14-16, 18-20, 22-24,
  27, 30-32, 34, 39, 41-42, 44,
  46, 54, 60, 70, 81, 83, 115

Morcanry, 17

Morean, 18

Moss, 21, 37, 50, 52-53, 57, 97,
  116-117

Mucklebury (Mickleberry), 60-61,
  63, 70-71, 73, 75, 77, 80

Muffett, 15-16, 18-20, 113

Muis, 107

Mulrunce, 14

Murphy (Murfey, Murphey), 6-7, 14,
  22, 74, 97, 105

Murray, 22, 27, 117, 119, 121

Muschet, 74, 76-78, 81, 83, 86-87,
  93, 95, 101-102, 116

N

Nally, 60

Nash, 46-47, 120

Neale, 8, 66-68, 71, 79, 81

Nelson, 69, 71

Nesbett (Nisbett, Nisbitt), 8,
  10, 13-23, 25, 27, 30-32, 35,
  42, 46, 48-50, 52-53, 57, 59-60,
  62, 107, 121-122, 124

Nevil, 78-79

Newman, 40

Noland (Nowland), 36, 38-39

Norman, 35

Norris, 33, 35

North, 8

Northcutt, 48

O

Obryan, 7

Oden, 34, 38

Oldham, 33, 42

Oliver, 74

Oneale, 72

Overall (Overhal), 33, 50, 107, 115

Overy, 52

Owins (Owings), 6, 69, 71, 73, 75

P

Parker, 4, 6, 8-9, 11, 13, 16, 18-20, 35, 107

Parris (Paris, Parish), 69, 71, 73, 75, 77, 80, 84, 89

Parsons, 24, 59-61, 63-64, 66

Pasons, 17

Pate, 79, 81

Patterson, 24, 27

Payne, 31

Peake, 69, 71, 74, 77, 112-113

Peils, 17

Peyne, 114

Peyton (Payton), 1-15, 17-18, 20-29, 31-34, 39-40, 42-60, 62, 79, 85-86, 102, 112, 115, 117, 123

Pickril, 70

Pierce (Pearce, Peirce), 28-29, 31, 33, 35-36, 38, 40-41, 43-44, 46, 48-49, 52, 112

Pilcher, 35, 40-41, 43-44, 46, 48-50, 52-53, 55-56, 58-61, 63-64, 76

Plain, 21

Platt, 78, 80

Pope, 89, 94

Porter, 112

Posey, 19, 21-22, 59, 69, 71, 73, 75, 77, 80, 118

Potter, 56-58, 60-61, 63-64, 66, 76

Powell, 32

Price, 115

Pridmore, 74

Prince, 115

Suthard, 59

Switman, 118

T

Tackett (Tacket), 9-10, 14, 40,
66, 111, 113

Taylor, 82, 95

Tebbs (Tibbs), 8-9, 11-13,
15-29, 31-34, 36-37, 39-49,
51-54, 56-57, 107-110, 114,
117, 123-124

Thayer (Thayor, Thyer), 28,
30-31, 33, 35, 48, 55, 57,
59-61, 63-64, 66

Thomas, 59, 63, 111, 119-120

Thompson (Tompson), 4, 46, 108

Thornton, 5, 123

Thurman, 6, 8-9, 11-14, 16-17,
19-20, 22, 24, 26, 43, 47, 65,
106, 109-111

Tingle, 74, 76, 81, 89, 91, 95

Tippitt, 3

Tolford, 52

Tomblin, 17

Tompkins (Tomkins), 31-32

Triplett (Triplet), 7, 9, 48

Turley, 117

Turner, 19, 50, 69, 71, 73, 75,
77, 81

Tuttle, 43

Twillaven, 50

Tyler, 38, 41

V

Van Eventon, 33

Vaughan, 120

W

Wagener (Waganer, Waggener), 3,
6, 8-9, 14, 16

Wagonage, 102

Waite (Wait, Wiat, Wyatt), 15-16,
18-20, 22-23, 25-26, 70, 119

Walden, 29, 32

Walker, 24, 26, 29, 31, 33-34, 71

Ward, 16

Washington, 67-68

Waters (Watters, Wayters), 6-7,
9, 11, 17-19, 29, 31, 33, 83,
107

Watkins, 24

Wearings, 103

Weaver, 78, 81

Webb, 14

Webster, 70-71, 76

Weedup (Wedup, Woodup), 3-4, 6
 8-9, 11, 24, 27-28, 30-31, 33,
 40

Wells (Wels), 17, 37, 40-41,
 43-44, 46, 48, 119

West, 74

Whailey (Whaley), 8, 33, 38

Wheeler, 82

White, 32, 56, 103, 117

Whitefield, 57, 84

Whitledge, 107, 112, 119, 123

Whitley, 9-10

Whittling, 10

Wickliffe (Whitlife, Whitliff,
 Wickliff), 8-9, 11-18, 20-23,
 67-68, 123-124

Wigginton, 35, 89-90, 92, 95, 97

Wikley (Wilky), 46, 48, 50,
 52-53, 55-58, 63, 66, 70, 89

Wilfred, 117

Wilkerson, 81-82, 89

Williams, 34, 40, 45, 52, 54-56,
 58, 60-64, 66, 69-71, 73, 75,
 78-80, 84-85, 88, 90-92, 98,
 102, 114, 116, 119-122

Williamson, 63, 65

Willow (Wello, Wilo), 20, 22, 24,
 26-29, 31-39, 41-46, 48-50,
 52-53, 69, 71, 73, 76

Wilson, 30, 37, 47

Wise, 36, 38-39, 41-45

Wiver, 124

Wood, 58, 69, 71, 73-75, 77, 80,
 89

Wright, 32, 56, 58-61, 70, 123

Wyre, 88

Y

Young (Youngs), 4, 6, 8, 14, 16,
 27, 74, 106-107, 117

At a Vestry called and held for the parish of Cittengen in the house of Mr. Wm. Tebbs in Dumfries 5th of September 1785

Present the Reverend Spence Grayson Minister, Henry Lee & Howson Hooe Churchwardens John Hooe, Wm. Alexander, John Kincheloe, Richd. Neale, Henry Washington Isaac Wickliffe & _____ Vestrymen

The Vestry do Recommend to each of the Members of Vestry to Advance to Colo. Jesse Ewell Eight Shillings & four pence apiece to be paid by him to the Legates sent from the Convention of the Protestant Episcopal Church to the General Convention which are shortly to meet in Philadelphia

It is Recommended also that the further sum of Eight Shillings & four pence be paid by the Vestry to Colo. Jesse Ewell for his Expences in Convention

The Vestry do Unanimously Appoint Colo. Jesse Ewell their Delegate to Represent them in the Next General Convention of the Protestant Episcopal Church

Ordered that the Several members of the Vestry hand about Subscriptions & make Collections for the Support of the Protestant Episcopal Church, & also Subscriptions to be offer'd for the Support of the Minister

Ordered that Colo. Henry Lee & William Alexander wait on _____ Bullett & take such Security for Six hundred Pounds left by _____ Jones Deceased to the Vestry of Cittengen parish as the said Jones Will Directs & Settle the Interest thereof

Signed {

Spence Grayson Minister

Henry Lee }
Howson Hooe } Churchwardens

John Hooe

Wm. Alexandor
John Kincheloe
Richd. Neale
Henry Washington
Isaac Wickliffe
and
Thomas Guthrie
} Gentn.
of the
Vestry

www.ingramcontent.com/pod-product-compliance
Lightning Source LLC
Chambersburg PA
CBHW070758290326
41931CB00011BA/2058